EASY WRITING: TEACHING STUDENTS HOW TO WRITE MORE COMPLEX SENTENCE STRUCTURES

Wanda C. Phillips, Ed.D.

Easy Grammar Systems Inc.

7717 E. Greenway Road

Scottsdale, AZ 85260

www.easygrammar.com

© 1990

Printed in the United States of America

EASY WRITING: TEACHING STUDENTS HOW TO WRITE MORE COMPLEX SENTENCE STRUCTURES is dedicated to my three wonderful children, Jenny Phillips, Peter Phillips, and Micah Phillips. I love you!

TABLE OF CONTENTS

A LETTER TO THE TEACHER...1

IMPORTANT NOTE...2

WHY TEACH **HOW** TO WRITE SENTENCE STRUCTURES............................3

IN PREPARATION...4

HOW TO TEACH *EASY WRITING*...5

SUGGESTIONS FOR HELPING STUDENTS IMPROVE WRITING SKILLS.................8

THE PROCESS OF WRITING..11

EFFECTIVE TEACHING..14

LEVEL 1

ANSWER KEY...397

UNIT I   **ITEMS IN A SERIES**..15
              ANSWER KEY..399

UNIT II   **SEMICOLON CONSTRUCTION.**......................................51
              ANSWER KEY..405

UNIT III   **APPOSITIVES.**..67
              ANSWER KEY..408

UNIT IV   **PARTICIPIAL PHRASES: PRESENT PARTICIPLE
              CONSTRUCTION**..77
              ANSWER KEY..409

UNIT V   **PARTICIPIAL PHRASES: PAST PARTICIPLE
              CONSTRUCTION**...101
              ANSWER KEY..413

UNIT VI   *HAVING* **+ PAST PARTICIPLE CONSTRUCTION**.................129
              ANSWER KEY..421

UNIT VII   **SUBORDINATE CLAUSES**...149
              ANSWER KEY..425

UNIT VIII   **RELATIVE CLAUSES**..169
                 ANSWER KEY..429

APPENDIX A: EDITING SYMBOLS...391

APPENDIX B: IRREGULAR VERBS..393

LEVEL 2

ANSWER KEY...433

UNIT I   **ITEMS IN A SERIES**..193
               ANSWER KEY..435

UNIT II   **SEMICOLON CONSTRUCTION**..233
               ANSWER KEY..443

UNIT III   **APPOSITIVES**...249
               ANSWER KEY..446

UNIT IV   **PARTICIPIAL PHRASES: PRESENT PARTICIPLE
               CONSTRUCTION**...261
               ANSWER KEY..449

UNIT V   **PARTICIPIAL PHRASES: PAST PARTICIPLE
               CONSTRUCTION**...297
               ANSWER KEY..456

UNIT VI   ***HAVING*** + **PAST PARTICIPLE CONSTRUCTION**.....................331
               ANSWER KEY..463

UNIT VII   **SUBORDINATE CLAUSES**..359
               ANSWER KEY..469

UNIT VIII   **RELATIVE CLAUSES**...375
               ANSWER KEY..472

APPENDIX A: EDITING SYMBOLS...391

APPENDIX B: IRREGULAR VERBS..393

AUTHOR'S CONFESSION AND PLEA:

I must confess that preliminary pages of texts have often been cast aside or perused carelessly in my haste to teach. Ultimately, results would have been achieved more readily had I taken time to study those vital recommendations placed at the beginning of most textbooks.

Aware of the multitude of preliminary pages in *Easy Writing: Teaching Students How To Write More Complex Sentence Structures,* I have reviewed them several times. All information, I feel, is essential; therefore, no deletions have been made. I **implore** you to read **all introductory** pages! After doing so, you may begin with any unit you choose. However, the first pages of this text are requisite to the successful teaching of this text.

A LETTER TO THE TEACHER:

Dear Teacher,

Easy Writing has been designed to help students learn how to write specific sentence structures. Concepts, however, are presented hierarchically, teaching the easiest materials and progressing to more difficult concepts in a step-by-step manner.

Two levels have been included in this text. Level 1, for grades 4-6, has been placed at the beginning; **level 2**, for junior high, high school, and adult learning has been placed in the latter part.

You will note that I have been repetitious in many explanations. The rationale for this lies in the fact that each teacher will use the materials differently. For those who will teach a unit straight through on a daily basis, the repetition is, actually, not necessary. Those teachers may wish to ignore the instruction included in each lesson. Other teachers will choose to use the materials only once or twice a week (or even month); for the students of those teachers, it is invaluable to have the concepts repeated. Although methods used to teach *Easy Writing* may vary, I feel that repetition is vital. After completing a unit, always ask students to write examples from previous units and to incorportate concepts into their writing. This process helps to insure mastery.

Finally, let me address the age-old issue of writing versus grammar. Many grammarians believe that grammar is of paramount importance. Writing theorists often claim that writing is unequivocally significant. Having written both *Easy Grammar* texts and *Easy Writing*, I believe both are equally essential. With a synthesis of the two, optimum language learning occurs.

Wanda C. Phillips

1

IMPORTANT MESSAGE:

You will note that usually two lessons are included for each discreet skill. In fact, identical information has been presented in both lessons. This has been done for a variety of reasons. First, some teachers will choose to teach and practice using the first lesson and then assign the second lesson for homework. Since students are likely to throw away the lesson done in class, it is vital for students to have this information presented again when they complete a homework assignment. Whereas some teachers will choose to teach *Easy Writing* as a unit of study, others will prefer to do a lesson (in sequence, I hope) just one or two days a week. For the latter, the repetition of the concept previously studied is imperative. If you find that the lesson presented is redundant, you, of course, may choose to skip the instructional part and go directly to the part of the lesson where students actually compose sentences. Last, as a teacher, I have often complained that, though texts frequently present concepts well, too few worksheets are supplied to reinforce the concept. Hopefully, presenting so many will enable some teachers to choose not to use every worksheet while giving others the abundance they need to adequately help students learn the concept.

928-767.
4000

2

WHY TEACH *HOW* TO WRITE SENTENCE STRUCTURES:

"Why must I teach sentence structure writing? Shouldn't students automatically know them?" are two questions often asked. The answer, a usual one in education, is that it depends on the child. Because higher level reading involves many higher level sentences, those students usually assimilate these structures. If students come from homes where oral sentence patterns reflect higher structure, they, too, will be more apt to write higher level sentences. Of course, in the classroom, one will find pupils who by nature are gifted in language; these students practically learn any language concept readily.

Many students, however, need to be taught **how** to write various sentence structures. *Easy Writing* has been designed to help students learn how to write specific sentence structures. Taught correctly, these materials will help to develop written expression. Keep in mind that these concepts need to be taught, with the teacher providing instruction, modeling patterns, providing active participation, monitoring student writing, and establishing an enthusiastic atmosphere. With patience, guidance, and much encouragement, students can be motivated to write more intricate sentence structures.

The terminal objective is for the student to be able to write the specific structure introduced in each unit. However, to teach these in isolation is senseless. **Practice** and **application** in the student's own writing is mandatory. Provide such experiences. Offering students opportunities for successful writing experiences will aid in achieving the ultimate reason for teaching how to write higher level sentence structures, that of instilling the joy of composition.

For effective teaching strategies, please refer to page 14.

HOW TO TEACH *EASY WRITING*:

1. You will note that I have been repetitious in many explanations. The rationale for this lies in the fact that each teacher will use the materials differently. For those who will teach a unit straight through on a daily basis, the repetition is, actually, not necessary. Those teachers may wish to dismiss the instruction included in each lesson. Other teachers will choose to use the materials only once or twice a week (or even month); for the students of those teachers, it is invaluable to have the concepts repeated. Although methods used to teach **Easy Writing** may vary, I feel that repetition is vital. After completing a unit, always ask students to write examples from previous units and to incorporate concepts into their writing. This process helps to insure mastery.

2. After you have finished a unit, be sure to apply it to your assigned compositions. For example, after introductory participial phrases have been learned, assign as a competency, the inclusion of one in a particular writing assignment. For mastery purposes, I suggest that this "targeted competency" occur many times during the school year.

3. Students need to become aware of different sentence structures used in all types of writing (novels, short stories, magazine articles, etc.). At the end of each unit, a page for recording sentence structures found in students' reading materials has

been provided. Students will write the sentence for that particular structure and the title of the specific work in which the sentence appears. You will need to determine how many pages you need to reproduce for your students and how specific the student must be in writing the source. (Some teachers may require only the name of a magazine whereas others will require the title of the article with the name of the magazine. Some teachers may also request the issue and/or page number as well.)

4. Be flexible. Teach *Easy Writing* in a manner that lends itself to your own teaching style, to your students' needs, and to the modes used to achieve previous success. Your teaching should reflect your enthusiasm for writing.

SUGGESTIONS FOR HELPING STUDENTS IMPROVE WRITING SKILLS:

1. **Encourage students to read.** Reading has a direct influence on writing ability. As a child reads at a higher level, sentence structure becomes more complex. Therefore, the student internalizes more complex writing without it being taught directly. Also, the more one reads, the better he becomes at it.

2. **Teach students grammar.** I know that this is not a popular idea, but I believe we can teach concepts along with writing. If a student understands capitalization usage, for example, he will not be burdened while writing. Many are of the notion that attention to mechanics and usage hampers creativity. Nonsense!

3. **Converse with students in complete sentences.** The more we articulate using more complex sentence structures and higher vocabulary, the more likely students are to assimilate these and use them in speaking **and** writing.

4. **Vocabulary improvement should be an ongoing process**. Seek out specific lessons for teaching new words. Also, teach prefixes, suffixes, and roots as vehicles for word comprehension.

5. **Give students ample opportunities to write.**

6. **Save students' work from previous years to serve as models.** Read them orally or pass them around for individual reading. Students need to know what you perceive as excellent.

7. **Use at least one sentence combining activity daily.** *Daily Grams: Guided Review Aiding Mastery Skills* contains 180 reviews with sentence combining activities. (See various levels on last page of this text.) Give students the opportunity to write their sentence combinings on the board or to share them orally. This gives you the chance to discuss various ways to write in higher level structures as well as providing for class editing.

> **Note:** Offer much praise. If you criticize sentence combinings, students
>
> may not want to share in the future. You want writing to be a
>
> wonderful experience. It's fine to show where a change may
>
> be necessary; however, positive reinforcement is mandatory.

8. **Be sure that students know their intended audience.** A junior high student would write very differently if he were writing a short story for kindergartners versus writing research to be shared with peers.

9. **Be sure that each student knows with whom he will be sharing his writing.** Writing can be very personal. Making someone read his presentation or even sharing it in an editing group may be an invasion of his privacy. Be sensitive to your students' needs.

10. **Let students see you enjoying the writing process, too!**

IN PREPARATION:

It is recommended that each student have the following items in preparation for *Easy Writing* instruction:

A.   an enthusiastic teacher who will share a love for writing

B.   an atmosphere where mistakes are not an embarrassment

C.   a dicitonary

D.   a thesaurus

E.   a composition book

For effective teaching strategies, please refer to page 14.

THE PROCESS OF WRITING:

Textbook companies should be praised for their excellent presentation of the steps of the writing process. These steps should be presented here as a review and for the purpose, in a few areas, of expansion.

STEP 1:   **Discussion**

Before beginning the actual task of writing, a discussion of the topic should occur. When more than one person participates in this activity, the sharing of ideas is called *brainstorming*. Students should be encouraged to jot down ideas. (Also, intended audience should be discussed.)

Occasionally, students are asked to individually list as many ideas as possible. This method is called *mindstorming*.*

STEP 2:   **Writing the rough draft**

In this step, students write their first copy. Many teachers suggest that children write a free flow of thoughts, not worrying about mechanics and grammar usage. Others, on the other hand, propose that all elements be a concern. (I lean more toward the latter proposition.)

Note: I suggest that the first draft be written in pencil on every other line. Editing and revision space is, thus, available. I also recommend that editing marks be done in pen because they are more readily seen.

STEP 3:   **Editing and revising**

The editing stage involves deletions, additions, and revisions. Students should have a list of editing symbols. (See Appendix A.)

*Credit given to Anthony Robbins.

Peer Review: This process precedes actual "hands-on" editing. Each student reads his entire rough draft to a "buddy." Then, the listener provides feedback, sharing if the writer has maintained his topic, used descriptive words, etc. The listener may ask questions to help the writer see inconsistencies or make additions that would make the writing more lucid.

The second part of peer review requires the writer to read the composition sentence by sentence. This time, the "buddy" listens for fragments and run-ons. (Asking students to stop at the end of each sentence facilitates this process.)

Editing: A number of editing procedures have been introduced.

1. **Peer editing:**

    Peer editing can be done in a number of ways. One method involves two students exchanging papers and searching for any errors or necessary changes. Of course, editing groups may consist of any number of students the teacher deems necessary.

Note: I place five students into every editing group and assign each a task. One student is assigned (or volunteers) to correct capitalization on all five rough drafts. Another person is given spelling errors. The other three students are assigned punctuation, grammar usage, and *all* (all of the above, plus topic sentence, margins, sentence variety, word choice, etc.), respectively. Delegating discreet tasks makes it easier for students to focus their editing. I use an editing form which students write at the end of their own rough draft. Each student is expected to write the following data:

_____	C	(capitalization)
_____	P	(punctuation)
_____	sp.	(spelling)
_____	gram.	(grammar usage)
_____	all	(topic sentence, margins, and all areas)

After correcting another student's rough draft, each person is required to place his initials in the space of the assigned area. Only when all spaces contain initials is he allowed to proceed to the next step of the writing process.

2. **Teacher-Student Editing:**

A conference occurs in this form of editing. This, an ideal situation, allows for explanation of errors and suggestions for revising. The only obstacle to teacher-student conferencing is the time factor, finding enough time to service each student.

Note: Some teachers, I am told, require two rough drafts, the first involving peer editing and the second including teacher conferencing. If this is your choice, I recommend a few days between each writing so that the students are not overwhelmed.

Revising: Revision of papers can occur simultaneously with editing. For example, if one who is editing finds a fragment, he can point it out to the writer and help him to correct it. Revising can also occur before or after the editing process with the purpose of identifying and correcting fragments, run-on sentences, awkward or confusing sentences, combining sentences into higher level structures, using better transitional words and phrases, adding vivid details, etc.

STEP 4: **Writing the published copy**

The final written copy is referred to as the published copy. Although this copy is the one a student may choose to share with a particular audience, it does not imply that the work will be sent to a publishing company.

13

EFFECTIVE TEACHING:

1. Make your **examples** lively, and, if possible, **relating to your students' interests and/or activities**. This will maintain interest and promote enthusiasm for writing.

2. Teach students to **embellish** their writing.

   Example: A squirrel ran across the lawn.

   Embellished Example: A **fat, quarrelsome** squirrel ran across the **moist, weed-filled** lawn.

   Good writing evokes vivid pictures. In this unit, as you read sentences that lend themselves well to embellishment, have the students do so. Teach students to use their senses to make their writing descriptive and appealing.

3. **Vocabulary expansion is imperative**. This can be accomplished both in direct vocabulary teaching, and, of course, in actual writing. As you find words in this unit that can be replaced by improved vocabulary, teach this concept.

   Example: A fat, quarrelsome squirrel **ran** across the lawn.

   Improved Example: A fat, quarrelsome squirrel **scampered** across the lawn.

3. **Effective teaching** often follows a set pattern.

   a. Focus (telling students what they are about to learn)

   b. Introduction (actual teaching)

   c. Guided practice (having students practice the concept taught)

   d. Ending (finishing the lesson by checking for understanding)

For additional examples, see page 194.

UNIT I

ITEMS IN A SERIES

For effective teaching strategies, please refer to page 14.

Name_____   **SUBJECTS IN A SERIES**

Date_____

In learning to improve our writing skills, we will sometimes join subjects. The **subject** of a sentence is **who** or **what** the sentence is about.

> **Example:**   The pilot talked to us.

We are talking about a *pilot*. *Pilot* is the subject of the sentence.

Sometimes, we talk about two things.

> **Example:**   The pilot and his dad talked to us.

We are talking about the pilot **and** his dad. *Pilot* **and** his *dad* are the subject of the sentence. We call this a **compound subject**. Usually, we use **and** to combine two words in a compound subject.

> **Example:**   Tom laughed at the clown. Carol laughed at the clown, too.
>
> Tom and Carol laughed at the clown.

Directions: Use **and** to join subjects of the two sentences.

1.   Bill walked to school. Susan walked to school, too.

_____

_____

2.   Some baby rabbits are in the field. Deer are also in the field.

_____

_____

17

3. Paper fell to the floor. A blue pen fell to the floor, too.

_____

_____

4. Her dad played baseball. Her mom played baseball, also.

_____

_____

5. This plant grew fast. This tree also grew fast.

_____

_____

6. The girls began to sing. The boys began to sing, too.

_____

_____

7. Dick jumped on a hay wagon. Sally jumped on a hay wagon, too.

_____

_____

8. Tom will go to the library. I will go to the library, also.

_____

_____

Name_____

Date_____

The **subject** of a sentence is **who** or **what** the sentence is about.

   Example: Her hair is brown.

We are talking about *hair*. *Hair* is the subject of the sentence. We place one line under the subject of the sentence.

   Example: Her <u>hair</u> is brown.

Sometimes, we talk about two things.

   Example: Her hair and eyes are brown.

We are talking about her hair **and** eyes. *Hair* **and** *eyes* are the subject of the sentence. We call this a **compound subject**. We place one line under each subject.

   Example: Her <u>hair</u> and <u>eyes</u> are brown.

In this lesson, we will combine sentences. We will also join two subjects with **and**.

   Example: This hat has holes. This shirt has holes, too.

   <u>This hat and shirt have holes.</u>

   Note: The verb *has* is used with one item.
      Example: This hat **has** holes.
   When we are talking about more than one item, the verb *have* is used.
      Example: This <u>hat</u> and <u>shirt</u> **have** holes.

Directions: Use **and** to join subjects of the two sentences.

1.   Cars zoomed down the street. Trucks zoomed down the street, too.

_____

_____

2.   Jody read a short story. Dave read a short story, too.

_____

_____

3.   Ann dropped popcorn on the floor. I also dropped popcorn on the floor.

_____

_____

4.   A small cup had been broken. A big plate had been broken, too.

_____

_____

5.   Blue paint had spilled on the rug. Glue had also spilled on the rug.

_____

_____

6.   Mark played basketball. Tammy played basketball, too.

_____

_____

The **subject** of a sentence is **who** or **what** the sentence is about.

Sometimes, we talk about two things.

> **Example:**   A <u>lion</u> and a <u>tiger</u> are in the jungle.

We are talking about a lion **and** a tiger. *Lion* **and** *tiger* are the compound subject of the sentence. Usually, we use **and** to combine subjects. We place one line under each subject of the sentence.

Sometimes, three or more things make up the subject.

> **Example:**   A <u>lion,</u> a <u>tiger,</u> and an <u>elephant</u> are in the jungle.

Directions: Use **and** to join subjects of the sentences.

1.   A red airplane took off. A large jet took off, too.

_____

_____

2.   Mary stepped on gum. Dick stepped on gum. I also stepped on gum.

_____

_____

3. His uncle has a van. His aunt has a van, too.

_____

_____

4. Mrs. Jones baked pies. Her husband baked pies. Their sons baked pies, too.

_____

_____

5. Barbara visited London Bridge. Her mother also visited London Bridge.

_____

_____

6. Their bikes blocked the door. Their skates blocked the door. Their scooters blocked the door, too.

_____

_____

7. A horse has a long tail. A cow also has a long tail.

_____

_____

The **subject** of a sentence is **who** or **what** the sentence is about. Sometimes, we talk about two or more things. *Or* can also be used to join a compound subject.

>   **Example:**   <u>Megan</u> **or** her <u>sister</u> will help us.

A verb may change form with a compound subject.

>   **Example:**   Your hand is muddy.   Your foot is muddy.

>   <u>Your hand and foot are muddy.</u>

We are talking about your hand **and** foot. *Hand* **and** *foot* are the compound subject. We place one line under each subject of the sentence.

>   Your <u>hand</u> and <u>foot</u> are muddy.

> **Note:**   Let's talk about the verb *is*. If the subject names only one thing (like hand), we use *is*.

>   **Example:**   Your <u>hand</u> <u>is</u> muddy.

>   Sometimes, we will talk about more than one. (More than one is called **plural**.) We, then, use the verb *are* to replace *is.*

>   **Example:**   Your <u>hands</u> <u>are</u> muddy.

Directions: Use *and* or *or* to join subjects of the sentences.

1.   Ed is always happy.   Donna is always happy, too.

_____

_____

2. Jack called to me. Josh called to me. Mike called to me.

_____

_____

3. Sam ate all the cookies. Jill may have eaten all the cookies.

_____

_____

4. A mother hen crossed the road. Her little chicks also crossed the road.

_____

_____

5. Their brother is a good cook. Their sister is a good cook.

_____

_____

6. Her dad may drive us to the game. Her mom may drive us to the game.

_____

_____

7. Her feet hurt from the long walk. Her ankles hurt from the long walk, too.

_____

_____

The **subject** of a sentence is **who** or **what** the sentence is about.

> **Example:**   Judy crossed the street.

We are talking about Judy. *Judy* is the subject of the sentence.

Sometimes, we talk about two things.

> **Example:**   Judy and her brother crossed the street.

We are talking about Judy and her brother. *Judy* and her *brother* are the subjects.
We call this a compound subject.

The verb of a sentence often tells **what happens** or **what happened**.

> **Example:**   Judy and her brother crossed the street.

Crossed tells what happened. We call this **past tense** because it already happened.

Sometimes the verb tells what is happening **now**.

> **Example:**   Tommy eats fudge.

The verb *eats* tells what is happening. We call this **present tense**.
At this point, it is not important to remember which tense we are using. However, when
we combine items, the verb sometimes changes slightly.

> **Example:**   Tommy **eats** fudge.   Liz **eats** fudge.
> Tommy and Liz **eat** fudge.

When the subject is one item or person, we usually add **s** to the verb if the sentence
tells what is happening now.

Examples: A <u>swan</u> <u>swims</u> on the lake.

Jay's <u>dad</u> <u>brings</u> home groceries.

<u>She</u> <u>talks</u> loudly.

When we are talking about more than one item in the present (happening now), we do **not** add <u>s</u> to the verb.

    Examples: A <u>swan</u> and a <u>duck</u> <u>swim</u> on the lake.

<u>Swans</u> <u>swim</u> on the lake.

Jay's <u>dad</u> and <u>mother</u> <u>bring</u> home groceries.

<u>Mr. Clay</u> and <u>she</u> <u>talk</u> loudly.

Directions: Write the verb in the space provided.

1.   Harry likes to dive. Jim also likes to dive.

Harry and Jim _____ (like, likes) to dive.

2.   Birds _____ often. (chirps, chirp)

3.   The mother dog barks at me. Her puppy barks at me, too.

The mother dog and her puppy _____ (bark, barks) at me.

4.   A bell rings. A telephone rings, also.

A bell and a telephone _____ (rings, ring).

5.   Ice cubes _____ (melt, melts).

6.   Todd sleeps on a cot. His sister sleeps on a cot, too. Todd and his sister

_____ (sleep, sleeps) on cots.

26

Name_____   **SUBJECTS IN A SERIES**

Date_____

Directions: Use **and** to join the subject of each sentence.

1.   That lady gives food to the needy. Her father also gives food to the needy.

_____

_____

2.   Bob takes piano lessons. Bob's grandpa takes piano lessons.

_____

_____

3.   The toy boat floats in the water. The rubber duck floats, too.

_____

_____

4.   Carl likes to fish at Hornet Lake. Tina likes to fish at Hornet Lake, also.

_____

_____

IMPORTANT NOTE: As previously stated, you may not need to do every lesson. Monitor and adjust to fit the needs of your students.

The **subject** of a sentence is **who** or **what** the sentence is about. Sometimes, we have only one subject.

>   **Example:**   That <u>car</u> looks shiny.

Sometimes, we have two subjects.

>   **Example:**   A <u>brush</u> and <u>comb</u> are on the table.

We are talking about a brush **and** comb. *Brush* **and** *comb* are the subject of the sentence. (We call this a compound subject.)

Sometimes, we have three or more subjects. This is a compound subject, also. When three items are placed in a row (series), place a comma (**,**) after each of the first two items.

>   **Example:**   <u>Shoes</u>, <u>sandals</u>, and <u>sneakers</u> lay on the floor.

We are talking about *shoes*, *sandals*, and *sneakers.* These are the compound subject of the sentence.

>   **Note:**   If we have a singular subject (one item), our verb will be different when
>   talking about present time.
>>   **Examples:**   <u>Tommy</u> play**s** ball.
>>   <u>Tommy</u> and <u>Jay</u> play ball.
>>   The <u>boys</u> play ball.

Directions: Use *and* to join subjects of these sentences.

1.   Fred likes to skate. Lisa likes to skate. Kim likes to skate, too.

_____

_____

2. A dog plays in the yard. A cat plays in the yard. A little girl plays in the yard.

   _____

   _____

3. A park will be built here. A zoo will be built here. A house will be built here.

   _____

   _____

4. Candy is sweet. Ice cream is also sweet. Cake is sweet, too.

   _____

   _____

5. Joy goes to dance lessons. Molly goes to dance lessons. I go to dance lessons.

   _____

   _____

6. A bell rang. An alarm rang. A telephone rang, too.

   _____

   _____

7. Miss Jay wears glasses. Mrs. Loe wears glasses. Mr. Dunn also wears glasses.

   _____

_____

Two items can be joined with *and*.

> **Example:**   The hill is steep. It is also smooth.
>
>   The hill is steep and smooth.

Three items can be placed together with *and*.

> **Example:**   Mary ate candy. Mary ate pie. Mary ate cake.
>
>   Mary ate candy, pie, and cake.

> **Note:**   When three items are placed in a row (series), place a comma (,)
> after each of the first two items.

Directions: Use *and* to join items in these sentences.

1.   Peter hit the ball hard. He hit the ball far.

_____

_____

2.   Uncle Don poured milk into his coffee. Uncle Don poured sugar into his coffee.

_____

_____

3. The sun is large. The sun is bright. The sun is also hot.

   _____

   _____

4. Jack read a book. Jack read a magazine, too. Jack also read a newspaper.

   _____

   _____

5. Lynn turned on the radio. She turned on the television, too.

   _____

   _____

6. Nancy ran into the house. She ran down three steps. She ran out the back door.

   _____

   _____

7. The teacher looked sad. The teacher also looked worried.

   _____

   _____

8. Erin bought a doll. Erin also bought a baton. She bought a mirror, too.

   _____

   _____

The subject of a sentence is **who** or **what** the sentence is about.

> **Example:** Birds flew away.

We are talking about birds. *Birds* is the subject of the sentence. We place one line under the subject.

> **Example:** <u>Birds</u> flew away.

Sometimes, we talk about two things.

> **Example:** <u>Birds</u> and <u>bats</u> flew away.

We are talking about birds **and** bats. *Birds* and *bats* are the subject of the sentence. (We call this a compound subject.) We place one line under each subject.

We may choose to use *both* before the first subject.

> **Example:** **Both** <u>birds</u> **and** <u>bats</u> flew away.

We may choose to use *not only* in front of the first subject. If we use *not only*, we need to use *but also*.

> **Example:** **Not only** <u>birds</u> **but also** <u>bats</u> flew away.

Directions: In Part A, use *and* to join the subject of each sentence. In Part B, write the sentence again using *both...and*.

1. Todd walked to school. Beth walked to school.

Part A: _____

Part B: **Both**_____

2. Those roses are pretty. The tulips are also pretty.

    Part A: _____

    Part B: **Both** _____

3. Her rings are on that chest. Her earrings are on that chest.

    Part A: _____

    _____

    Part B: **Both** _____

    _____

4. A large ship sailed into the bay. A small boat sailed into the bay, also.

    Part A: _____

    _____

    Part B: **Both** _____

    _____

5. A notebook is under your bed. Pencils are also under your bed.

    Part A: _____

    _____

    Part B: **Both** _____

    _____

The subject of a sentence is **who** or **what** the sentence is about.

> **Example:** Milk had been spilled on the counter. Juice had been spilled on the counter, too.
>
> <u>Milk</u> **and** <u>juice</u> had been spilled on the counter.

We are talking about two things that were spilled. We call this a compound subject.

We may use *both* in front of the first subject. ***Both-and*** are called correlative conjunctions.

> **Example:** **Both** milk **and** juice had been spilled on the counter.

We may choose to use *not only* in front of the first subject. If we use *not only*, we need to use *but also*.

> **Example:** **Not only** milk **but also** juice had been spilled on the counter.

Directions: Write the boldfaced words in each sentence.

1.   The **apples** and **pears** are rotten.

Part A: Both the _____ and _____ are rotten.

Part B: Not only the _____ but also the _____ are rotten.

2. The **girls** and **boys** learned to sew.

    Part A: Both the _____ and _____ learned to sew.

    Part B: Not only the _____ but also the _____ learned to sew.

3. The **house** and the **barn** had been flooded by heavy rains.

    Part A: Both the _____ and the _____ had been flooded by heavy rains.

    Part B: Not only the _____ but also the _____ had been flooded by heavy rains.

4. **Billy** and his **mother** helped with the pumpkin sale.

    Part A: Both _____ and his _____ helped with the pumpkin sale.

    Part B: Not only _____ but also his _____ helped with the pumpkin sale.

5. **Robins** and **sparrows** chirped in our pine tree.

    Part A: Both _____ and _____ chirped in our pine tree.

    Part B: Not only _____ but also _____ chirped in our pine tree.

The subject of a sentence is **who** or **what** the sentence is about.

    Example: A deer looked at us.

We are talking about a deer. Deer is the subject of the sentence.
Sometimes, we talk about two things. We usually join two things with *and*.

    Example: A deer and a rabbit looked at us.

We are talking about two things: a *deer* and a *rabbit*.

We may use **both** in front of the first subject. **Both-and** are called correlative conjunctions.

    Example: **Both** a deer **and** a rabbit looked at us.

We may choose to use **not only** in front of the first subject. If we use **not only**, we need to use **but also**.

    Example: **Not only** a deer **but also** a rabbit looked at us.

Directions: In Part A, join the two subjects with *and*. In Part B, rewrite the sentence.

    Example: Paper fell from her purse. Pencils fell from her purse.

         Part A: Paper and pencils fell from her purse.

         Part B: **Both** paper and pencils fell from her purse.

1.   An owl sat in a tall oak tree. A swallow sat in a tall oak tree.

    Part A: _____

    _____

Part B: **Both** _____

_____

2.   Rob ate breakfast. His friend ate breakfast, too.

Part A: _____

_____

Part B: **Both** _____

_____

2.   A squirrel played on the lawn. A chipmunk also played on the lawn.

Part A: _____

_____

Part B: **Both** _____

_____

4.   Joey ran to the swings. Mindy also ran to the swings.

Part A: _____

_____

Part B: **Both** _____

_____

When we join subjects, we may use *and*.

> **Example:**   His leg hurt. His arm hurt.
>
> _____His leg **and** arm hurt._____

When we join subjects, we may use *both* in front of the first subject.

> **Example:**   _____**Both** his leg **and** arm hurt._____

When we join subjects, we may use *not only...but also*.

> **Example:**   _____**Not only** his leg **but also** his arm hurt._____

Directions: In Part A, join the two subjects using *both*. In Part B, join the subjects using *not only...but also*.

1.   Pizza will be served. Tacos will also be served.

Part A: **Both** _____

_____

Part B: **Not only** _____

_____

2.   Her family came to the party. Her friends came to the party, too.

Part A: **Both** _____

_____

Part B: **Not only** _____

_____

3. A mailman came to our door. A salesman came to our door.

Part A: **Both** _____

_____

Part B: **Not only** _____

_____

4. A fly flew around them. A bee also flew around them.

Part A: **Both** _____

_____

Part B: **Not only** _____

_____

5. Nick won a contest. His older sister also won.

Part A: **Both** _____

_____

Part B: **Not only** _____

_____

When we join subjects, we may use ***and***.

        Example: The girls talked to the coach. The boys talked to the coach.

                The girls **and** boys talked to the coach.

When we join subjects, we may use ***both*** in front of the first subject.

        Example: **Both** the girls **and** boys talked to the coach.

When we join subjects, we may use ***not only...but also***.

        Example: **Not only** the girls **but also** the boys talked to
                the coach.

ő ő ő ő ő ő ő ő

Directions: In Part A, join the two subjects using *both*.
                   In Part B, join the subjects using *not only...but also*.

1.   Pins were on the floor. Needles were on the floor, too.

    Part A: **Both**_____

    Part B: **Not only**_____

    _____

2.   Dave ate steak. Paul also ate steak.

    Part A: **Both**_____

Part B: **Not only** _____

_____

3.   Mrs. Thomas knitted sweaters. Mr. Thomas knitted sweaters.

Part A: **Both** _____

Part B: **Not only** _____

_____

4.   This buzzer rang loudly. That alarm also rang loudly.

Part A: **Both** _____

Part B: **Not only** _____

_____

5.   Her friend left early. Her sister left early, too.

Part A: **Both** _____

Part B: **Not only** _____

_____

6.   Jan looked strangely at me. Bob also looked strangely at me.

Part A: **Both** _____

Part B: **Not only** _____

_____

42

Name_____   **COMBINING ITEMS USING**
                                              OR
Date_____

Sometimes, we can join two items by using *or.*

       Example: I want to feed a rabbit. I may want to feed a squirrel instead.

          __I want to feed a rabbit **or** a squirrel.__

Directions: Join two items with or.

1.   Pam drives a car. She might drive a van.

_____

2.   Joe decided to swing. He may have decided to slide.

_____

3.   The family is going to a lake. The family may go to the river instead.

_____

_____

4.   Those cups are dirty. They may be tea-stained.

_____

ADDITIONAL WRITING SPACE

The subject of a sentence is **who** or **what** the sentence is about.

>   **Example:**   Her <u>car</u> is new.

Sometimes, we talk about two items. We can join them with *or* if it makes sense.

>   **Example:**   This <u>hat</u> **or** <u>scarf</u> is made of silk.

We are talking about a hat **or** a scarf. Because only one item could be made of silk, we use *or* instead of *and*.

You may use **either...or**. Put the word *either* in front of the first subject and *or* before the second.

>   **Example:**   **Either** this <u>hat</u> **or** this <u>scarf</u> is made of silk.

Directions: The compound subject has been joined by *or* in Part A.
              In Part B, use *either* in front of the first subject.

1.   Part A: <u>Your penny or your dime is under the table.</u>_____

     Part B: _____

              _____

2.   Part A: <u>A cup or a dish has been broken.</u>_____

     Part B: _____

              _____

3.   Part A: <u>A toy or a game had been given as a prize.</u>

      Part B: _____

               _____

4.   Part A: <u>A kite or a paper airplane could be made in art class.</u>

      Part B: _____

               _____

5.   Part A: <u>Miss Hobbs or Mr. Flint teaches Sunday school.</u>

      Part B: _____

               _____

6.   Part A: <u>My aunt or uncle will take us to the zoo.</u>

      Part B: _____

               _____

7.   Part A: <u>Flower seeds or pumpkin seeds are planted there.</u>

      Part B: _____

               _____

8.   Part A: <u>Sparky or some birds ate the dog food.</u>

      Part B: _____

Date_____

The subject of a sentence is **who** or **what** the sentence is about.

Example: This <u>tree</u> is old.

Sometimes, we talk about two items. We can join them with *or* if it makes sense.

Example: The <u>Crows</u> or <u>Cardinals</u> won.

We are talking about the Crows and the Cardinals. Because only one team could win, we use *or* instead of *and*.

You may use *either...or*. Put the word *either* in front of the first subject.

Example: **Either** the <u>Crows</u> **or** the <u>Cardinals</u> won.

Directions: The compound subject has been joined by *or* in Part A.
In Part B, use *either* in front of the first subject.

1. Part A: <u>Milk or tea will be served.</u>_____

   Part B: _____

   _____

2. Part A: <u>Bob or Joy lives there.</u>_____

   Part B: _____

   _____

3.   Part A: Crayons or colored pencils may be used. _____

      Part B: _____

                _____

4.   Part A: My mom or dad will make lunch. _____

      Part B: _____

                _____

5.   Part A: Shoes or sandals must be worn. _____

      Part B: _____

                _____

6.   Part A: A dog or cat ran into our house. _____

      Part B: _____

                _____

7.   Part A: Mark or his sister is first on the slide. _____

      Part B: _____

                _____

Name_____   **ITEMS IN A SERIES**

Date_____

As you read, you will note that authors have used these sentence structures in their writing. Find examples. Write each example and its source (where you found it).

Sentence: _____

_____

Source: _____

Sentence: _____

_____

Source: _____

Sentence: _____

_____

Source: _____

Sentence: _____

_____

Source: _____

Sentence: _____

_____

Source: _____

Sentence: _____

_____

Source: _____

Sentence: _____

_____

Source: _____

Sentence: _____

_____

Source: _____

Sentence: _____

_____

Source: _____

50

UNIT II

SEMICOLON CONSTRUCTION

For effective teaching strategies, please refer to page 14.

A semicolon is a comma with a period above it (;). A semicolon joins two thoughts that are about the same thing (topic). The two thoughts joined by a semicolon must be complete thoughts. That means that each thought could stand alone as a sentence.

We must make sure we understand if a group of words says a complete thought.

Examples: <u>This puppy has a cute nose.</u>   (**complete thought**)
                                               (**sentence**)

                  <u>When our dad came home.</u>   (**not a complete thought**)
                                          (**not a sentence**)

(We have a subject [<u>dad</u>] and a verb [<u>came</u>].

However, we don't know what happened when Dad came home.)

                  <u>Ran down the street.</u>   (**not a complete thought**)
                                      (**not a sentence**)

(We do not know *who* ran down the street. We are missing a subject.)

Directions: Write **S** in the blank if the group of words says a complete thought.
              Write **NS** in the blank if the group of words does not say a complete thought.

1. _____   Their sister plays soccer.

2. _____   If you leave.

3. _____   In the afternoon.

4. _____   A jump rope is on the floor.

5. _____ After you eat lunch.

6. _____ The trees in the winter.

7. _____ A monkey can be fun to watch.

8. _____ Sending a smoke signal.

9. _____ Debra and her mother.

10. _____ Your money is on the counter.

11. _____ Some flowers in the garden.

12. _____ Before the race began.

13. _____ Swimming in the lake.

14. _____ The man in the blue suit.

15. _____ She paints nearly every day.

REVIEW: A semicolon may be used to join two complete thoughts. A complete thought can stand alone as a sentence. We place a semicolon (;) after the first complete thought. We must remember that the two thoughts must be about the same topic. The word after a semicolon is not capitalized.

Directions: Read the sentences. Draw a happy face in the blank if the topic is the same before and after the semicolon. Draw a sad face if the sentences are not about the same topic.

1. _____ Jill likes to read; candy is on the table.

2. _____ Ken's grandpa sent a gift; it is a saddle.

3. _____ The girls went on a hike; this needle is too little.

4. _____ Her joke was funny; everybody laughed.

54

A sentence says a complete thought. You may wish to join two complete thoughts with a semicolon instead of using *and*.

> **Example:** My sister likes to talk, <u>and</u> she is always on the telephone.
>
> <u>My sister likes to talk; she is always on the telephone.</u>

The two thoughts (sentences) joined by a semicolon must be about the **same** topic.

> **Correct:** <u>The lion lay in the grass; her cub slept beside her.</u>
>
> **Wrong:** <u>The lion lay in the grass; we like pizza.</u>

Did you notice that the word following a semicolon is not capitalized?

Sometimes we will place <u>therefore</u> or <u>however</u> after the semicolon if it makes sense.

> **Examples:** <u>I like ice cream; **therefore**, I'll take three scoops.</u>
>
> <u>I like ice cream; **however**, I don't want any now.</u>

NOTE: Place a comma **after** the words *therefore* and *however*.

Directions: Use a semicolon (;) to join the two sentences. Use *therefore* and *however* in sentences where it tells you to include them.

1. Her kitten is playing. He is chasing a ball.

_____

_____

2. We rode on a new bus. It is red and blue.

_____

_____

3. Kent will not go. I will not go either. (Use <u>therefore</u>.)

_____

_____

4. The bag tore. A can of soup fell on the floor. (Use <u>therefore</u>.)

_____

_____

5. Sam and Nan love math. They like to add the most.

_____

_____

6. I love turkey. I dislike the dark meat. (Use <u>however</u>.)

_____

_____

7. That pencil will not work. You may use mine. (Use <u>however</u>.)

_____

_____

A sentence says a complete thought. You may wish to join two complete thoughts with a semicolon (;) rather than *and*.

> **Example:** This bow doesn't match; I'll use that red one.

The two complete thoughts (sentences) joined by a semicolon must be about the **same topic**.

> **Correct**: My brother likes cherry pie; my sister likes coconut cream pie.

These sentences are about desserts. We say they are about the same topic.

> **Wrong:** My brother likes cherry pie; this rock is smooth.

These thoughts are not about the same topic.

Sometimes we will place words like *therefore* or *however* after the semicolon if it makes sense.

NOTE: Place a comma after words like *therefore* and *however*.

> **Examples:** Mrs. Smith is nice; **therefore**, we like her.
>
> Ginny fell off the swing; **however**, she wasn't hurt.

Directions: The first complete thought has been written. Place a semicolon and write another complete thought about the same topic. (Place a comma after *therefore* or *however*.)

1. Their keys are lost   **therefore**_____

_____

2. <u>We want to go</u>   **however** _____

_____

3. <u>Cotton candy is good</u>   **however** _____

_____

4. <u>We won the game</u>   **therefore** _____

_____

5. <u>Her hair was sticky</u>   **therefore** _____

_____

6. <u>Mark is small for his age</u>   **however** _____

_____

7. <u>A glass broke</u>   **therefore** _____

_____

8. <u>They like to camp</u>   **therefore** _____

_____

9. <u>That is my best teddy bear</u>   **however** _____

_____

A sentence says a complete thought. You may wish to join two complete thoughts with a semicolon instead of using *and*.

> **Example:** We are going to the lake, <u>and</u> we will take a picnic lunch.
>
> <u>We are going to the lake; we will take a picnic lunch.</u>

The two thoughts (sentences) joined by a semicolon must be about the same topic.

> **Correct:** <u>Use this towel; those are dirty.</u>
>
> **Wrong:** <u>Use this towel; the rock is red.</u>

Sometimes we will place words like <u>therefore</u> or <u>however</u> after the semicolon if it makes sense.

> **Examples:** <u>I like cheese pizza; **however**, I like pepperoni better.</u>
>
> <u>The game is at 2 P.M.; **therefore**, you need to come by noon to</u>
>
> <u>get ready.</u>

Directions: The first complete thought has been written. Place a semicolon and write another complete thought about the same topic.

1. <u>This milk is sour</u>_____

_____

2. A parade came down the street _____

_____

3. It rained all day _____

_____

4. The teacher is happy _____

_____

5. Jan picked up a ball _____

_____

6. His dad likes to cook _____

_____

7. This floor is dirty _____

_____

8. Today is very cold _____

_____

9. A bus stopped at the corner _____

_____

60

A sentence is a complete thought. A complete thought has a subject and a verb. The subject is who or what the sentence is about. The verb tells what happens or what is.

Sentence: The bus stops here.

We are talking about a *bus*. *Stops* tells what the bus does or what happens to the bus. You may want to join two complete thoughts. Sometimes you use *and*. You may also use a semicolon instead of *and*.

NOTE: A semicolon (;) looks like a comma with a period above it.

Examples: Sandy plays soccer, and her mom is the coach.

Sandy plays soccer; her mom is the coach.

To use a semicolon, you must have two **complete** thoughts and they must be about the **same** topic.

Correct: Pam leaned against the gate, and she tried to move it.

Pam leaned against the gate; she tried to move it.

Wrong: Pam leaned against the gate; her sister likes to read.

Directions: The first complete thought has been written. Place a semicolon after it, and write another complete thought about the same topic.

1. Dogs are fun_____

_____

2.   My friend is nice

3.   This bike is broken

4.   Sally drew a picture

5.   These fries are cold

6.   Ken opened the door

7.   This teddy bear is soft

8.   Mom's birthday is this week

Name_____   **SEMICOLON**
                                           CONSTRUCTION
Date_____

A semicolon joins two thoughts that are about the same topic. The two thoughts

joined by a semicolon must say a complete idea. That means that each thought

could stand alone as a sentence if we wanted.

    Example: <u>The tire is flat; we need to pump it.</u>

Directions: The first complete thought has been written. Place a semicolon
              (;) after that thought and write another complete thought about
              the same topic.

    Example: <u>It rained for two days; the streets were flooded.</u>

1. <u>A parade marched by</u>_____

_____

2. <u>Your shoe is on the floor</u>_____

_____

3. <u>Jane asked a question</u>_____

_____

4. <u>Trash is all over the street</u>_____

_____

5. The train stopped suddenly _____

_____

6. Today is very hot _____

_____

7. James is sitting in the corner _____

_____

8. The player ran to the end of the field _____

_____

9. This apple pie smells good _____

_____

10. Larry's aunt will visit next week _____

_____

11. Todd wrote a letter _____

_____

12. This book has many pictures _____

_____

As you read, you will note that authors have used semicolons in their writing. Find examples. Write each example and its source (where you found it).

Sentence: _____

_____

Source: _____

Sentence: _____

_____

Source: _____

Sentence: _____

_____

Source: _____

Sentence: _____

_____

Source: _____

Sentence: _____

_____

Source: _____

Sentence: _____

_____

Source: _____

Sentence: _____

_____

Source: _____

Sentence: _____

_____

Source: _____

Sentence: _____

_____

Source: _____

UNIT III

APPOSITIVES

EFFECTIVE TEACHING:

Refer to page 14.

Name_____   **APPOSITIVES**

Date_____

An appositive is a group of words that explains something in a sentence.

     Example: His pet, *that tiny turtle*, is under the chair.

An appositive is placed next to the word it explains.

     Example: Kim has a toy, *a pink and blue top*.

An appositive is set off by commas.

     Example: Joanie, *my best friend*, likes to skate.

Directions: Place the appositive by the word it explains.

     Example: Fluffy is their cat. Fluffy is black and white.

     Fluffy, **their cat**, is black and white._____

1.   Dr. Hand is my dentist. Dr. Hand looks at my teeth.

  Dr. Hand _____ looks at my teeth._____

2.   Harry went to Globe. Globe is a town in Arizona.

  Harry went to Globe _____

3. The farmer stood next to Millie. Millie is a cow.

    The farmer stood next to Millie _____

4. Katy is a good softball player. Katy hit a home run.

    Katy _____ hit a

    home run. _____

5. Troy is my cousin. Troy is on the track team.

    Troy _____ is on the track team. _____

6. Linn bought a drink. The drink was a banana milkshake.

    Linn bought a drink _____

7. His mother is an artist. His mother draws horses.

    His mother _____ draws horses. _____

8. This book is a science fiction novel. This book is Ted's.

    This book _____ is Ted's. _____

9. Pat shared his lunch. His lunch was a peanut butter and jelly sandwich.

    Pat shared his lunch _____

    _____

An appositive is a group of words that explains something in a sentence.

   Example: My pet, ***this cuddly rabbit***, is soft.

"This cuddly rabbit" explains your pet. Without it, the sentence would read: "My pet is soft." We would have no idea what kind of a pet the person has. *This cuddly rabbit* **explains** the kind of pet.

An appositive is placed next to the word it explains.

   Example: I like that **dessert**, ***the strawberry pie***.

The strawberry pie explains which dessert the person likes.

The group of words about the pie is placed next to the word, dessert.

An appositive is set off by commas.

   Example: Joel's **grandpa**, <u>an artist</u>, painted this picture.

Directions: Place the appositive by the word it explains.

   Example: Miss Baker is their piano teacher. Miss Baker is nice.

   <u>Miss Baker**, their piano teacher,** is nice.</u>

1.   Todd's uncle gave me a gift. It was a yellow kite.

   <u>Todd's uncle gave me a gift_____</u>

_____

2. This book is a mystery. This book is good.

   This book   is good.

3. His favorite food is pizza. It will be served for lunch.

   His favorite food   will be served for

   lunch.

4. Cindy is my friend. Cindy lives next door.

   Cindy   lives next door.

5. Sparky is a puppy. Sparky licks my hand.

   Sparky   licks my hand.

6. Lalita is my aunt. Lalita is visiting us.

   Lalita   is visiting us.

7. The desserts are pie and cake. The desserts are on the table.

   The desserts   are on the table.

8. Mom won a prize. It is a red and white dish.

   Mom won a prize   .

9. Mrs. Barnes gave me a sticker. Mrs. Barnes is a Sunday school teacher.

   Mrs. Barnes   gave me a sticker.

72

Date_____

An appositive is a group of words that explains something in a sentence.

   Example: My sister, *the girl with the pigtails*, likes cats.

An appositive is placed next to the word it explains.

   Example: We like that **dog**, *the one with brown spots.*

An appositive is set off by commas.

   Example: A colt, *a baby horse*, has wobbly legs when born.

Directions: Place the appositive by the word it explains.

   Example: A robin is a bird. A robin is a sign of spring.

              A robin, **a bird**, is a sign of spring.

1.   Fido is my dog. Fido likes to chew bones.

      Fido_____ likes to chew bones._____

2.   Bob is my brother. Bob races cars.

      Bob_____ races cars._____

3. Joan is Sandy's friend. Joan lives in New York.

    Joan _____ lives in New York. _____

4. He rode Mr. Carter's horse. The horse is a brown mare.

    He rode Mr. Carter's horse _____ .

5. The building was torn down. The building was an orange barn.

    The building _____ was torn down. _____

6. Mr. Reed comes to visit us. Mr. Reed is our minister.

    Mr. Reed _____ comes to visit us. _____

7. Fluffy is a French poodle. Fluffy jumps around too much.

    Fluffy _____ jumps around too much. _____

8. Timmy ate fruit for lunch. He ate two apples and a pear.

    Timmy ate fruit _____ for lunch. _____

9. Two stuffed animals are on the bed. They are a bear and a pig.

    Two stuffed animals _____ are on the bed. _____

Name_____   **APPOSITIVES**

Date_____

As you read, you will note that authors have used appositives in their writing. Find examples. Write each example and its source (where you found it).

Sentence: _____

_____

Source: _____

Sentence: _____

_____

Source: _____

Sentence: _____

_____

Source: _____

Sentence: _____

_____

Source: _____

Sentence: _____

_____

Source: _____

Sentence: _____

_____

Source: _____

Sentence: _____

_____

Source: _____

Sentence: _____

_____

Source: _____

Sentence: _____

_____

Source: _____

76

UNIT IV

PARTICIPIAL PHRASES
PRESENT PARTICIPLE CONSTRUCTION

EFFECTIVE TEACHING:

Refer to page 14.

One type of participial phrase is made using the present participle of the verb. The present participle is formed by adding **ing** to a verb.

Examples: to stand = _standing_

                     to stop   = _stopping_

                     to like   = _liking_

Directions: Write the present participle for each verb.

Example: to run - _running_

1.	to find	_____	11.	to pass	_____
2.	to dance	_____	12.	to meet	_____
3.	to pull	_____	13.	to ask	_____
4.	to bake	_____	14.	to stir	_____
5.	to spend	_____	15.	to let	_____
6.	to tap	_____	16.	to know	_____
7.	to speak	_____	17.	to throw	_____
8.	to live	_____	18.	to finish	_____
9.	to make	_____	19.	to cry	_____
10.	to see	_____	20.	to shout	_____

ADDITIONAL WRITING SPACE

A participial phrase is formed by adding **ing** to a verb and placing a few words with it.

> **Example:**   sitt**ing** on a fence

Pattern: *present participle + word or words*

> **Example:**   fixing his bike   =   fixing   +   his bike
>   **present   words**
>   **participle**

A phrase is made up of more than one word. In this pattern, we have a present participle plus a word or words. Therefore, we call this particular construction a participial phrase.

Because we will place the participial phrase at the beginning of a sentence, we call it an **introductory** participial phrase.

𝓫 𝓫 𝓫 𝓫 𝓫

Directions: The present participle has been written for you. Add a word or words (phase) to the present participle.

> **Example:**   going **to a fair**

1.   hopping _____

2.   running _____

3.   playing _____

4.   reading _____

5.   flying _____

6. eating _____

7. picking _____

8. hiding _____

9. washing _____

10. taking _____

11. sending _____

12. opening _____

13. hitting _____

14. being _____

15. writing _____

16. laughing _____

17. planting _____

18. riding _____

19. falling _____

20. looking _____

21. sleeping _____

22. smiling _____

23. drinking _____

The present participle is formed by adding <u>ing</u> to the verb. A phrase is simply a group of words. A participial phrase must have at least two words.

   Example: <u>Look**ing** sad</u>

Introductory means that the participial phrase is placed at the beginning of the sentence. The pattern becomes:

   present participle + word(s) + comma + subject + rest of sentence

   Example: <u>Look**ing** sad, the *collie* licked my hand.</u>

Collie is the subject because it tells what the sentence is about.

Directions: Combine the two sentences into one new sentence using an introductory participial phrase.

   Example: The man turns the key. He unlocked the door.

   <u>Turning the key, the man unlocked the door.</u>

1.   A small child was eating pizza. The small child burned his lip.

   _____

   _____

2.   The teller counted the money. The teller talked about her vacation.

   _____

   _____

3.   Sandy and Todd fished in a stream. Sandy and Todd caught three trout.

_____

_____

4.   Bobby stopped the car. Bobby checked the tires.

_____

_____

5.   Jill made pancakes. Jill flipped one in the air.

_____

_____

6.   Helen was smelling pepper. Helen sneezed.

_____

_____

7.   The girl is lying on the floor. The girl is reading a magazine.

_____

_____

Introductory participial phrases follow three rules:

> **Rule 1:**   An <u>ing</u> verb will be the first word of the sentence.
>
> **Rule 2:**   The <u>ing</u> verb must have at least one other word with it to make it a phrase (group of words).
>
> **Rule 3:**   The participial phrase must be placed first in the sentence.

Introductory means that the participial phrase is placed at the beginning of a sentence.

To write a sentence beginning with an introductory participial phrase, follow this pattern:

> **Pattern:**   **Present participle + word(s) + comma + subject + rest of sentence**

> Note: The subject is <u>who</u> or <u>what</u> the sentence is about.

comma

> **Example:**   **Filling** a bag with chips, <u>Peter</u> packed his lunch.
>   present   phrase   subject   rest of sentence
>   participle

Directions: A participial phrase, a comma, and the subject have been written for you. Finish each sentence.

> **Example:**   <u>Hopping on foot, Barry and Lee **crossed the finish line.**</u>

1.   <u>Looking for his jacket, Brian</u>_____

_____

2.   Pretending to be a duck, Patty _____

_____

3.   Trying to climb a hill, the hiker _____

_____

4.   Sharing her lunch, Barbara _____

_____

5.   Hanging a poster in his room, Scott _____

_____

6.   Chewing gum, the bus driver _____

_____

7.   Petting his kitten, the boy _____

_____

8.   Sitting on the bank of a stream, the fisherman _____

_____

9.   Hoping for a red wagon for her birthday, Julie _____

_____

Introductory participial phrases follow three rules:

Rule 1: An <u>ing</u> verb will be the first word of the sentence.

Rule 2: The <u>ing</u> verb must have at least one other word with it to make it a phrase (group of words).

Rule 3: The participial phrase must be placed first in the sentence.

A verb plus the <u>ing</u> ending is called the present participle.

Examples: to sneeze = **sneezing**

to watch = **watching**

A participial phrase = present participle + word(s)

Examples: sneezing suddenly

watching for his father

Pattern: present participle + word(s) + comma + subject + rest of sentence

Example: Sneezing suddenly, our best <u>friend</u> closed her eyes.

present   word comma   subject   rest of sentence

participle

Directions: The participial phrase, a comma, and the subject have been written for you. Complete each sentence.

Example: <u>Watching television, I **ate a sandwich and munched on**</u>

popcorn._____

1. <u>Sitting in a chair, Miss Blake</u>_____

_____

2.   Reaching for a cookie, the little boy _____

   _____

3.   Skating on a frozen pond, Missy _____

   _____

4.   Setting the table, Timmy _____

   _____

5.   Playing a game of softball, we _____

   _____

6.   Hearing its name called, the puppy _____

   _____

7.   Hanging a picture on the wall, their parents _____

   _____

8.   Making a sandwich, Mike _____

   _____

A participial phrase may be formed by adding <u>ing</u> to a verb and adding a word or words.

A. The present participle is formed by adding <u>ing</u> to the verb.

Example: to drink = drinking

B. A phrase is a group of words.

Example: **drinking a glass of water**

An introductory participial phrase is placed at the beginning of a sentence. **After an introductory participial phrase, place a comma (,), the subject, and the rest of the sentence.**

Remember: A subject is *who* or *what* the sentence is about.

Example: Drinking water hurriedly, I spilled it on my shirt.

        ð ð ð ð ð

Directions: A participial phrase has been written for you. Write a comma, the subject, and the rest of the sentence.

Example: Combing her hair, **Jessica swept the sides back.**

1. Talking on the telephone _____

_____

2.   Diving off the board _____

_____

3.   Beating on a drum _____

_____

4.   Racing her bike _____

_____

5.   Waving to their friends _____

_____

6.   Tripping over a tin can _____

_____

7.   Walking in a parade _____

_____

8.   Making my own breakfast _____

_____

9.   Dropping her pencil _____

90   _____

A participial phrase may be formed by adding ing to a verb and adding a word or words.

    A.   The present participle is formed by adding ing to the verb.

        Example: to draw   =   **drawing**

    B.   A phrase is a group of words.

        Example: **drawing a picture**

An introductory participial phrase is placed at the beginning of a sentence. After an introductory participial phrase, place a comma (,), the subject, and the rest of the sentence.

Remember: A subject tells *who* or *what* the sentence is about.

    Example: Wading in a stream, the *child* giggled and splashed.

Directions: A participial phrase has been written for you. Write a comma, the subject, and the rest of the sentence.

    Example: Starting the car, **Mary put it into reverse.**

1.   Smiling at the baby _____

_____

2.   _Slipping on ice_ _____

_____

3.   _Writing on the wall_ _____

_____

4.   _Pulling a wagon_ _____

_____

5.   _Turning on the light_ _____

_____

6.   _Stopping the ball_ _____

_____

7.   _Playing tag_ _____

_____

8.   _Acting like a monster_ _____

_____

9.   _Leaning back in his chair_ _____

92   _____

Name_____   **PARTICIPIAL PHRASES**

Date_____

Participial phrases can be placed **after** the subject.

Remember: participial phrase   =   verb(ing)   +   word(s)

       Example: watch**ing some whales**

Pattern: **subject + comma + present participle (ing) + words +**

       comma + rest of sentence.

     Example: Her *bird*, **flying around the room**, couldn't find a place to land.

Directions: The subject, comma, and present participle have been written. Add
       a word or group of words to the present participle, place a comma,
       and finish the sentence.

     Example: This lemon, hanging **at the tree's top, was the biggest.**

1.   Jim, making _____

_____

2.   The club, choosing _____

_____

3.   Jane's dad, wearing _____

_____

4. <u>A policeman, helping</u> _____

    _____

5. <u>Mandy, smelling</u> _____

    _____

6. <u>Five boys, rushing</u> _____

    _____

7. <u>The baby, crying</u> _____

    _____

8. <u>A large spider, spinning</u> _____

    _____

9. <u>A student, thinking</u> _____

    _____

10. <u>Her pet sheep, following</u> _____

    _____

11. <u>A loud noise, sounding</u> _____

_____

You can begin a sentence with the subject. A subject tells **who** or **what** the sentence is about.

> **Example:**   Some <u>**turtles**</u> stopped.

We are talking about *turtles*. Therefore, *turtles* is the subject.

After the subject, we can place a present participle. A present participle adds <u>ing</u> to a verb.

> **Example:**   to crawl   =   crawl**ing**

If we add a word or group of words to the <u>ing</u> verb, a phrase is formed. A phrase is more than one word. Because the <u>ing</u> word is called a present participle, the phrase has a special name. It is called a participial phrase.

> **Example:**   **crawling** on a rock

For this sentence structure, we follow this pattern.

Pattern: **subject + comma + present participle + word(s) + comma + rest of sentence**

> Example: Some <u>turtles</u>, crawl**ing** on a rock, stopped.
>
>
>
> comma   comma
> subject   present   rest of sentence
> participle + phrase
>
>

𝕏 𝕏 𝕏 𝕏 𝕏

Directions: Two sentences have been written for you. Combine these into one sentence. Write your subject, a comma, a participial phrase, a comma, and the rest of the sentence.

> **Example:**   A moose was standing in the woods. The moose yawned.
>
> <u>A moose, standing in the woods, yawned.</u>

1. The dog is lying in the grass. The dog is chewing a bone.

   _____

   _____

2. A cat was eating food. The cat looked up.

   _____

   _____

3. The boy was playing baseball. The boy hit a home run.

   _____

   _____

4. Kirk's dad is washing his car. He is talking to his friend.

   _____

   _____

5. Miss Sands is looking for her lost hamster. Miss Sands appears upset.

   _____

   _____

You can begin a sentence with the subject. A subject tells **who** or **what** the sentence is about.

> **Example:**   A **bird** flew away.

We are talking about a <u>bird</u>. Therefore, <u>bird</u> is the subject.

After the subject, we can place a present participle. A present participle is formed by adding <u>ing</u> to a verb.

> **Example:**   to chirp   =   chirp**ing**

If we add a word or group of words to the <u>ing</u> verb, a phrase is formed. A phrase is more than one word. Because the <u>ing</u> word is called a present participle, the phrase has a special name. It is called a participial phrase.

> **Example:**   A <u>bird</u>, chirping softly, flew away.

ᚼ ᚼ ᚼ ᚼ ᚼ

Directions: Combine the two sentences using the above pattern.
Write the subject, a comma, the participial phrase, and the rest of the sentence.

Example: Grandpa is standing on the patio. He watches birds in the garden.

<u>Grandpa, sitting on the patio, watches birds in the garden.</u>

1.   The man is sitting in his truck. He is writing a letter.

_____

2.   Their sister was baking cookies. Their sister burned herself on the hot pan.

_____

_____

3.   The family is going on vacation. The family has the dog in the car.

_____

_____

4.   The child stood in the middle of the floor. The child was crying for his mother.

_____

_____

5.   Lana was laughing at her brother. Lana bumped into the wall.

_____

_____

Name_____

Date_____

As you read, you will note that authors have used present participle construction in their writing. Find examples. Write each example and its source (where you found it).

Sentence: _____

_____

Source: _____

Sentence: _____

_____

Source: _____

Sentence: _____

_____

Source: _____

Sentence: _____

_____

Source: _____

Sentence: _____

_____

Source: _____

ᕷ ᕷ

Sentence: _____

_____

Source: _____

ᕷ ᕷ

Sentence: _____

_____

Source: _____

ᕷ ᕷ

Sentence: _____

_____

Source: _____

ᕷ ᕷ

Sentence: _____

_____

Source: _____

UNIT V
PARTICIPIAL PHRASES
PAST PARTICIPLE CONSTRUCTION

For effective teaching strategies, please refer to page 14.

We will learn to write participial phrases beginning with the past participle. For our purposes here, we will work with regular verbs. These use another verb called a helping verb. (We will use *has, have,* or *had.*) To form the past participle of a regular verb, we add **ed** to the verb.

Examples:

	past	**past participle**
to talk	talked	(had) **talked**
to wish	wished	(had) **wished**
to stop	stopped	(had) **stopped**

ᵟ ᵟ ᵟ ᵟ ᵟ

Directions: Write the past participle of each verb.

Example: (to hop) Each child had __hopped__ on one foot for two minutes.

1. (to play) We had _____ for an hour.

2. (to fix) The girl has _____ her bike.

3. (to watch) They have _____ television for a long time.

4. (to paste) Nancy had _____ two papers together.

5. (to skip) She has _____ across the street.

6. (to love) Their aunt had _____ that book.

7.   (to clap)   Paul must have _____ for five minutes.

8.   (to lift)   The mother had _____ the baby from his crib.

9.   (to bake)   She had _____ a cake.

10.   (to hug)   The little girl has _____ her doll.

11.   (to park)   Dad has _____ the car.

12.   (to clean)   Tom has _____ his room.

13.   (to wash)   Miss Smith had _____ her hands and face.

14.   (to paint)   The classes have _____ pictures on a paper.

🍐 🍐 🍐 🍐 🍐

Directions: Draw a line from the verb to the past participle.

to bark	(had) rubbed
to hand	(had) laughed
to rub	(had) barked
to stop	(had) handed
to laugh	(had) stopped

We will learn to write participial phrases beginning with the past participle. For our purposes here, we will work with regular verbs. These use another verb called a helping verb. (We will use *has*, *have*, or *had*.) To form the past participle of a regular verb, we add *ed* to the verb.

Examples:

	past	**past participle**
to jump	jumped	(had) **jumped**
to yell	yelled	(had) **yelled**
to play	played	(had) **played**

Directions: Write the past participle of each verb.

Example: (to look) Zak has **looked** for his coat for a long time.

1.   (to paint)   She had _____ the wall green.

2.   (to chew)   Our dog has _____ his bone.

3.   (to jump)   He had _____ over a rock.

4.   (to cook)   Jill has _____ dinner.

5.   (to open)   Brad had _____ the gift.

6.   (to fish)   They had _____ in that stream several times.

7.   (to walk)   Their brother has _____ to the store.

8.   (to like)   Ryan had _____ the play.

9.   (to pretend) She had _____ to be asleep.

10. (to hand)   Her sister had _____ her friend a cola.

11. (to mop)   Katie has _____ the floor.

12. (to pat)   John and I have _____ that dog.

13. (to rest)   That tired worker has _____ for ten minutes.

14. (to press)   She had _____ her cheeks against the cold window.

15. (to rinse)   Dad has _____ mud off his truck.

ỗ ỗ ỗ ỗ ỗ

Directions: Draw a line from the verb to the past participle.

to spell   (had) kicked

to wrap   (had) printed

to dip   (had) believed

to kick   (had) wrapped

to print   (had) dipped

to believe   (had) spelled

106

The past participle of a **regular verb** is made by adding **ed**.

    Example: to scream = (had) scream**ed**

Some verbs do not add *ed* to form the past or past participle. These verbs are called

irregular verbs.

    Examples:

	past	past participle
to give	gave	(had) **given**
to sing	sang	(had) **sung**
to eat	ate	(had) **eaten**
to ride	rode	(had) **ridden**

Irregular verbs do not add ed to the past participle. Each irregular verb forms the past

participle differently. Your teacher will help you learn these.

        ŏ ŏ ŏ ŏ ŏ

Directions: Write the past participle of each verb.

    Example: (to rise) Smoke had __**risen**__ from the chimney.

1.   (to ride)   Amanda has _____ a horse.

2.   (to sing)   Three people have _____ a funny song.

3.   (to ring)   The bell has _____.

4.   (to give)   Has Bert _____ you his keys?

5.   (to send)   Grandpa has _____ a card.

6.   (to drive)   Miss Barnes had _____ to school.

7.   (to speak)   Edna has _____ loudly.

8.   (to eat)   We have _____ too much candy.

9.   (to fall)   Tim and I have _____ on the ice.

10.   (to steal)   Freddy has _____ third base.

11.   (to find)   They have _____ an old ring.

12.   (to see)   The conductor had _____ two men jump from the train.

13.   (to go)   A large boat had _____ around the harbor.

14.   (to choose)   The principal has _____ me to help.

15.   (to take)   He has _____ his sleeping bag along.

ᕚ ᕚ ᕚ ᕚ ᕚ

Directions: Draw a line from the verb to the past participle.

to freeze	(had) written
to throw	(had) known
to write	(had) frozen
to know	(had) thrown
to sit	(had) sat

108

A past participle form can be used to describe a noun (usually something you can see).

Examples: to fall   =   (had) **fallen**   ⇨   a **fallen** walnut

                 to close   =   (had) **closed**   ⇨   a **closed** door

                 to break   =   (had) **broken**   ⇨   the **broken** wagon

In our English language, we call a word that is formed from a verb and used as a describing word (adjective) a verbal.

ㅎ ㅎ ㅎ ㅎ ㅎ

Directions: Write the past participle of each verb. Then, write that word in the next space.

          Example: to surprise   =   __(had) **surprised**_____

                                   ⇨ _a___**surprised**___look_

1.   to park   =   __(had)_____

                 ⇨ _a_____ car

2.   to freeze   =   __(had)_____

                 ⇨ _a_____ pond

3.   to burn   =   __(had)_____

                 ⇨ _____ cookies

4. to steal   =   ___(had)_____

    ➪ _a_____ automobile

5. to write   =   ___(had)_____

    ➪ _a_____ message

6. to rent   =   ___(had)_____

    ➪ _that_____ vehicle

7. to rip   =   ___(had)_____

    ➪ _a_____ shirt

8. to lose   =   ___(had)_____

    ➪ _a_____ animal

9. to wrap   =   ___(had)_____

    ➪ _her_____ package

10. to fry   =   ___(had)_____

    ➪ _____ chicken

11. to sprain   =   ___(had)_____

    ➪ _a_____ ankle

110

A past participle form can be used to describe a noun (usually something you can see).

Examples:	to cook	=	(had) **cooked**	⇨	a **cooked** ham
	to wear	=	(had) **worn**	⇨	some **worn** shoes
	to pay	=	(had) **paid**	⇨	**paid** bills

In our English language, we call a word that is formed from a verb and used as a describing word (adjective) a verbal.

ᕮ ᕮ ᕮ ᕮ ᕮ

Directions: Write the past participle of each verb. Then write that word in the next space.

     Example: to pull   =   __(had) **pulled**_____

                                      ⇨ _a   **pulled**   muscle_

1.   to spill   =   __(had)_____

                               ⇨_____ milk

2.   to peel   =   __(had)_____

                               ⇨_____ potatoes

3.   to return   =   __(had)_____

                               ⇨ _a_____ letter

4. to hurt = <u>(had)</u> _____

   ⇨ <u>a</u> _____ <u>finger</u>

5. to fade = <u>(had)</u> _____

   ⇨ _____ <u>jeans</u>

6. to spoil = <u>(had)</u> _____

   ⇨ <u>a</u> _____ <u>child</u>

7. to tire = <u>(had)</u> _____

   ⇨ <u>the</u> _____ <u>hiker</u>

8. to cover = <u>(had)</u> _____

   ⇨ <u>a</u> _____ <u>wagon</u>

9. to scare = <u>(had)</u> _____

   ⇨ <u>a</u> _____ <u>person</u>

10. to pack = <u>(had)</u> _____

    ⇨ <u>a</u> _____ <u>lunch</u>

11. to soften = <u>(had)</u> _____

    ⇨ _____ <u>butter</u>

112

The past participle form used as a describing word (verbal) can be placed before the

noun it describes.

Example: to damage   =   _(had) **damaged**_

a   **damaged**   automobile

The verbal can also be placed at the beginning of a sentence. The pattern becomes:

past participle form (verbal) **+** a comma **+** the subject (noun described) **+** rest of

the sentence.

Example: _a   **damaged**   automobile_

___**Damaged**___, the _automobile_ was worth much less.
              comma

past participle   **subject**   **rest of sentence**

             🝆 🝆 🝆 🝆 🝆

Directions: Write the past participle of each verb in the first blank. Then, write that
same word in the next blank. *Be sure to read the second sentence.*

Example: to list

a ____**listed**____ number

___**Listed**___, the number was easily found in the telephone book.

1.   to comb

_____ hair

_____, his hair looked sharp.

113

2. to lock

a _____ gate

_____, the gate was a good way to keep out unwanted visitors.

3. to repeat

a _____ message

_____, the message was more easily understood.

4. to melt

_____ cheese

_____, the cheese oozed all over the plate.

5. to freeze

a _____ dessert

_____, the icy dessert hurt his teeth.

6. to steal

a _____ bike

_____, the blue bike had been found in the woods.

The past participle form used as a describing word (verbal) can be placed before the noun it describes.

Example: to paint   =   _(had)_ **painted**

_a_   **painted**   _bench_

Painted__, the old bench looked new.

When the past participle form used as a describing word (verbal) is placed as the first word in a sentence, we must follow this pattern:

**past participle   +   comma   +   subject   +   rest of sentence**

Example: __**Wrapped**__, the shiny _package_ was handed to the customer.
                                    comma
                past participle   **subject**   **rest of sentence**

ꙮ ꙮ ꙮ ꙮ ꙮ

Directions: Write the past participle of each verb in the first blank. Then, write that same word in the next blank. _Be sure to read the second sentence._

Example: to free

a _____**freed**_____ slave

__**Freed**__, former slaves started new, happier lives.

1.   to lose

a _____ dog

_____, the dog wandered through the streets.

115

2. to sprain

a _____ ankle

_____, her ankle swelled and hurt.

3. to relax

a _____ person

_____, Debra lay down on the floor to read.

4. to excite

an _____ child

_____, the child jumped up and down.

5. to cook

_____ vegetables

_____, the vegetables were soft and tasty.

6. to paint

a _____ face

_____, his face looked like a clown.

Name_____

Date_____

The past participle form used as an adjective (verbal) can be placed before the noun it describes.

Example: to fall   =   _(had) **fallen**_   ⇨   a **fallen** tree

We can also place the verbal at the beginning of a sentence and add a comma followed by the subject it describes.

Example: a **fallen** tree

Fallen, the tree spread its twisted limbs on the soft, moist earth.

The subject of this sentence is the noun, *tree*. *Tree* is what the sentence is about. *Fallen* is a describing word going over to (modifying) *tree*.

More Examples: a **torn** dress

Torn, the dress lay in a heap on the wicker chair.

a **finished** paper

Finished, the paper was handed to the teacher.

🪀 🪀 🪀 🪀 🪀

Directions: Write the past participle of each verb in the first blank. Then, write that same word in the next blank. *Be sure to read the second sentence.*

Example: to wash   a ____**washed**____ cup

____**Washed**____, the cup was put on a drain board.

1.   to write   a _____ message

_____, the message explained why Susie had been absent on Monday.

2. to raise

a _____ flag

_____, the flag waved in the wind.

3. to trust

a _____ friend

_____, the man was given a large sum of money to hold.

4. to fill

_____ stockings

_____, the stockings were heavy with gifts.

5. to break

a _____ wagon

_____, the wagon lay in pieces.

6. to hide

a _____ camera

_____, the camera takes pictures of people at the bank.

118

Name_____

Date_____

The past participle is part of the verb made by placing a helping verb in front of it. Usually, the helping verbs are *has*, *have*, or *had*.

Examples:	*Infinitive*	*Present*	*Past*	*Past Participle*
	to raise	raise(s)	raised	had **raised**
	to polish	polish(es)	polished	had **polished**
	to sing	sing(s)	sang	had **sung**
	to begin	begin(s)	began	had **begun**

Another way to write a sentence containing a past participle form is to add a group of words (phrase) to it.

Examples:	to raise	__(had) **raised**__
		__**Raised** on a farm__
	to sing	__(had) **sung**__
		__**Sung** off key__

A past participle plus a word or group of words (phrase) is called a participial phrase. To write a sentence using this, begin with a participial phrase, add a comma, write the subject (*who* or *what*), and the rest of the sentence.

Pattern: past participle + word(s) + comma + subject + rest of sentence

Examples: __**Raised** on a farm, the *boy* knows how to plow.__

__**Sung** off key, the *song* sounded terrible.__

🍐 🍐 🍐 🍐 🍐

119

Directions: In each sentence, the participial phrase has been written for you. Finish each sentence. *Be sure to place a comma after the phrase and write the subject next.*

Example: Given bubble gum, **Bob blew big bubbles.**

1. Taken to the principal _____

    _____

2. Locked in a car _____

    _____

3. Driven at a high speed _____

    _____

4. Followed by a mean dog _____

    _____

5. Made of wool _____

    _____

6. Thrown over the fence _____

    _____

7. Placed in a sink _____

    _____

The past participle is part of the verb made by placing a helping verb in front of it. Usually, the helping verbs are *has*, *have*, or *had*.

Examples:

Infinitive	*Present*	*Past*	*Past Participle*
to drop	drop(s)	dropped	had **dropped**
to follow	follow(s)	followed	had **followed**
to choose	choose(s)	chose	had **chosen**

Another way to write a sentence containing a past participle form is to add a group of words (phrase) to it.

Examples: to drop   <u>   (had) **dropped**   </u>

<u>   **Dropped** off at a park   </u>

to choose   <u>   (had) **chosen**   </u>

<u>   **Chosen** for a part in the play   </u>

A past participle plus a word or group of words (phrase) is called a participial phrase. To write a sentence using this, begin with a participial phrase, add a comma, write the subject (*who* or *what*), and the rest of the sentence.

Pattern: past participle   +   word(s)   +   comma   +   subject   +   rest of sentence

Examples: <u>**Dropped** off at a park, *he* played basketball.</u>

<u>**Chosen** for a part in the play, *Linda* was happy.</u>

🍐 🍐 🍐 🍐 🍐

Directions: In each sentence, the participial phrase has been written for you.   Finish
each sentence. *Be sure to place a comma after the phrase and write
the subject next.*

Example: Knocked down, **the small child began to cry**.

1.   Baked for a whole hour _____

_____

2.   Scrubbed clean _____

_____

3.   Chased by two girls _____

_____

4.   Chosen the winner _____

_____

5.   Taught how to swim _____

_____

6.   Yelled at for being late _____

_____

7.   Finished with their work _____

_____

A participial phrase may be started with the past participle + a word or group of words (phrase).

> **Example:** **Sent** to his mother

A participial phrase may be placed at the beginning of a sentence.

> **Example:** **Sent** to his mother, the card contained money and a thank you note.

A participial phrase may be placed at other places in a sentence.

> **Example:** The card, **sent** to his mother, contained money and a thank you note.

ᘓ ᘓ ᘓ ᘓ ᘓ

Directions: Complete each sentence.

1. The company, begun in 1960, _____

_____

2. The team, defeated again, _____

_____

3. Her dime, dropped on the floor, _____

_____

4. A rabbit, huddled in a corner, _____

5. The teacher, surprised by the students,

_____

6. His hair, brushed well,

_____

7. The cat, curled up on a bed,

_____

8. The book, read nightly,

_____

9. The car, broken down in the driveway,

_____

10. Their vacation, spent in a tent,

_____

11. Her birthday party, held at a pizza place,

_____

12. The dog, trained to shake hands,

_____

A participial phrase may be started with the past participle + a word or group of words (phrase).

      Example: **Stirred** slowly

A participial phrase may be placed at the beginning of a sentence.

      Example: **Stirred** slowly, the batter began to bubble.

A participial phrase may be placed at other places in a sentence.

      Example: The batter, **stirred** slowly, began to bubble.

Directions: Complete each sentence.

1.   The singers, led by Miss Smith, _____

_____

2.   A white cake, frosted with pink icing, _____

_____

3.   The dollar bill, torn into two pieces, _____

_____

4.   Candy, eaten before dinner, _____

_____

5.   Her hair, pulled back into a ponytail, _____

_____

6.   His sack lunch, laid on a chair, _____

_____

7.   A heart, carved out of wood, _____

_____

8.   A coat, found on the playground, _____

_____

9.   Cookies, decorated with red sprinkles, _____

_____

10.   The ball, hit to second base, _____

_____

11.   The child, reminded to do his chores, _____

_____

12.   Two pictures, pasted to a paper, _____

_____

Name_____

Date_____

As you read, you will note that authors have used past participle construction in forming participial phrases in their writing. Find examples. Write each example and its source (where you found it).

Sentence: _____

_____

Source: _____

Sentence: _____

_____

Source: _____

Sentence: _____

_____

Source: _____

Sentence: _____

_____

Source: _____

127

Sentence: _____

_____

Source: _____

Sentence: _____

_____

Source: _____

Sentence: _____

_____

Source: _____

Sentence: _____

_____

Source: _____

Sentence: _____

_____

Source: _____

128

UNIT VI

HAVING + PAST PARTICIPLE CONSTRUCTION

For effective teaching strategies, please refer to page 14.

130

We need to understand the past participle of a verb in order to write the "having"

construction. The past participle of a verb is formed in a regular verb by adding **ed**. To

decide the past participle form, place the word *had* in front of it.

> **Example:**   to brush   <u>had brush**ed**</u>

An irregular verb does not add <u>ed</u> to form the past participle. The entire word changes.

However, to decide the past participle form, still place the word *had* in front of it.

> **Example:**   to sing   <u>had **sung**</u>

If you are not sure if you should add <u>ed</u> to a verb or change its entire form, look in the

dictionary. If the verb is irregular and changes, it will give you the past participle form.

It may help you to take any verb and say the *present*, *past*, and then, *past participle*

using the helping verb, *had*.

Examples:

	present	past	past participle
to push	push(es)	pushed	(had) **pushed**
to walk	walk(s)	walked	(had) **walked**
to ring	ring(s)	rang	(had) **rung**
to go	go(es)	went	(had) **gone**

Directions: Write the past participle in the blank.

1.   (to walk)   They had _____ to the corner.

2. (to go) Her pet had _____ under the house.

3. (to yell) Some parents had _____ loudly to get their children's attention.

4. (to eat) A frog had _____ a fly.

5. (to pull) Sammy had _____ a wagon of hay.

6. (to sail) A large ship had _____ there.

7. (to smile) The clerk had _____ at me.

8. (to do) They had _____ their homework.

9. (to like) The baby had _____ his bath.

10. (to stay) Joan had _____ home.

11. (to leave) The bus had _____ .

12. (to see) We had _____ a spider.

13. (to hunt) They had _____ for the lost book.

14. (to tear) Her dog had _____ her paper.

15. (to find) Some boys had _____ a cave.

We need to understand the past participle of a verb in order to write the "having" construction. The past participle of a verb is formed in a regular verb by adding **ed**. To decide the past participle form, place the word *had* in front of it.

> **Example:**   to pull   _had pull**ed**_

An irregular verb does not add **ed** to form the past participle. The entire word changes. However, to decide the past participle form, still place the word *had* in front of it.

> **Example:**   to sit   _had **sat**_

If you are not sure if you should add **ed** to a verb or change its entire form, look in the dictionary. If the verb is irregular and changes, it will give you the past participle form.

It may help you to take any verb and say the *present*, *past*, and, then, *past participle* using the helping verb, *had*.

Examples:

	present	past	past participle
to scrub	scrub(s)	scrubbed	(had) **scrubbed**
to listen	listen(s)	listened	(had) **listened**
to drive	drive(s)	drove	(had) **driven**
to send	send(s)	sent	(had) **sent**

ő ő ő ő ő

Directions: Write the past participle in the blank.

1.   (to chase)   That goose had _____ after the others.

2.   (to smell)   Dan had _____ the pizza.

3.   (to give)   Her friend had _____ her a balloon.

4.   (to ride)   They had _____ their bikes all day.

5.   (to finish)   The class had _____ a short story.

6.   (to look)   We had _____ for the missing sock for ten minutes.

7.   (to print)   A man had _____ a sign.

8.   (to run)   Gary and Amy had _____ a race.

9.   (to break)   Andy had _____ a bottle.

10.   (to place)   She had _____ her name on the paper.

11.   (to fill)   Santa had _____ the stockings.

12.   (to cut)   I had _____ out a picture.

13.   (to drink)   Toby had _____ his milk.

14.   (to fold)   Mom had _____ the clothes.

The past participle is formed by adding **ed** to a regular verb.   The past participle form of an irregular verb does not add **ed**. It changes.

Examples: to love   _had **loved**_   (regular verb)

to write   _had **written**_   (irregular verb)

The past participle is decided by placing *had* in front of it.

Examples:

	present	**past**	**past participle**
to talk	talk(s)	talked	(had) **talked**
to steal	steal(s)	stole	(had) **stolen**

To use the "having" construction, first write ***having***. Then, add the past participle.

Examples: **having** talk**ed**

having stolen

After the past participle, we can place a word or phrase (group of words).

Example: Having stolen **a wallet**

Next, we add a comma, the subject (*who* or *what* we are talking about) and the rest of the sentence.

Example: Having stolen a wallet, **the _thief_ ducked into a store.**

ඊ ඊ ඊ ඊ ඊ

Directions: Write a past participle in the first blank. Then, complete the sentence.

Example: Having_____**read**_____a book, John_____**told**_____

his friend about the ending._____

135

1. Having _____ a nail, the girl _____

_____

2. Having _____ up a balloon, he _____

_____

3. Having _____ the ball, the batter _____

_____

4. Having _____ a rattle, the laughing baby _____

_____

5. Having _____ a toy car, Eric _____

_____

6. Having _____ money, the boy _____

_____

7. Having _____ for a day, the children _____

_____

8. Having _____ happily, they _____

_____

136

The past participle is formed by adding **ed** to a regular verb.   The past participle form of an irregular verb does not add **ed**. It changes.

Examples:	to frown	had **frowned**	(regular verb)
	to lie	had **lain**	(irregular verb)

The past participle is decided by placing *had* in front of it.

Examples:

	present	**past**	**past participle**
to see	see(s)	saw	(had) **seen**
to pray	pray(s)	prayed	(had) **prayed**

To use the "having" construction, first write **having**. Then, add the past participle.

Examples: **having seen**

having pray**ed**

After the past participle, we can place a word or phrase (group of words).

Example: Having seen a pretty sofa

Next, we add a comma, the subject (*who* or *what* we are talking about) and the rest of the sentence.

Example: Having seen a pretty sofa, **I am saving my money to buy it.**

ᶑ ᶑ ᶑ ᶑ ᶑ

Directions: Write a past participle in the first blank. Then, complete the sentence.

Example: Having   **bought**   a car, Mrs. Johnson

washed and waxed it.

1. Having _____ the game, the team _____

   _____

2. Having _____ a meal, Sarah _____

   _____

3. Having _____ his favorite teddy bear, the child_____

   _____

4. Having _____ the movie, the actress_____

   _____

5. Having _____ nuts, the squirrel _____

   _____

6. Having _____ all night, her dad _____

   _____

7. Having _____ some cereal, Ken _____

   _____

138

We can begin a sentence with the word, *having*, and add the past participle of a verb.

Example: **Having** cleaned   (verb: to clean)

After the past participle, we can place a comma and then the subject of the sentence.

Remember: The subject of a sentence is *who* or *what* the sentence is about.

Example: **Having** cleaned his room, *Josh* went out to play.

subject

The sentence is about *Josh*. Therefore, *Josh* is the subject. After the subject, place

the rest of the sentence telling what happens (happened) or what is (was). In the

example, *went out to play* is the rest of the sentence. It tells what happened.

Pattern: **Having** + past participle + word(s) + a comma + subject + rest of sentence

Directions: *Having*, the past participle, a word or phrase, a comma, and the subject
have been written for you. Complete each sentence.

Example: Having bowled three games, Mark **figured**

out his new average.

1.   Having made brownies, Larry and Sue _____

_____

2. Having stopped suddenly, Panya _____

    _____

3. Having eaten a banana split, Janice _____

    _____

4. Having fallen, I _____

    _____

5. Having swum all day, they _____

    _____

6. Having cooked dinner, Mother _____

    _____

7. Having earned twenty dollars, we _____

    _____

8. Having helped his grandmother, Steve _____

    _____

140

Name_____

Date_____

We can begin a sentence with the word, *having*, and add the past participle of a verb.

> **Example:** **Having** fallen (verb: to fall)

After the past participle, we can place a comma and then the subject of the sentence. Remember: The subject of a sentence is *who* or *what* the sentence is about.

> **Example:** **Having** fallen, the ***child*** cried.
>
> **subject**

The sentence is about a ***child***. Therefore, ***child*** is the subject. After the subject, place the rest of the sentence telling what happens (happened) or what is (was). In the example, *cried* is the rest of the sentence.

Pattern: **Having** + past participle + word(s) + a comma + subject + rest of sentence

𝄞 𝄞 𝄞 𝄞 𝄞

Directions: *Having*, the past participle, a word or phrase, a comma, and the subject have been written for you. Complete each sentence.

> **Example:** Having jumped, the horse **skidded into a pool of mud.**

1. Having yelled, the boy _____

_____

2. _Having found a quarter, the little girl_ _____

    _____

3. _Having done their homework, Bob and Tom_ _____

    _____

4. _Having washed his bike, Fred_ _____

    _____

5. _Having sung three songs, we_ _____

    _____

6. _Having tripped over a rock, Miss Hanks_ _____

    _____

7. _Having run out of the yard, the puppy_ _____

    _____

8. _Having taken a bath, the two children_ _____

    _____

9. _Having seen a snake, I_ _____

    _____

Now that you know how to form the past participle, we can practice using the "having" sentence structure.

Pattern: **Having** + past participle + word(s) + a comma + subject + rest of sentence

comma ↗

Example: **Having** practiced every day, *Stan* now plays better.

past participle   subject   rest of sentence

[phrase   ]

Directions: *Having*, the past participle, and words have been written for you. Place a comma, write a subject, and complete the sentence.

Example: Having tied his shoes, **Chad ran off to**

join his friends on the swings.

1.   Having washed all the windows _____

_____

2.   Having had a bad dream _____

_____

3.   Having scared their friend _____

_____

4. Having colored a picture _____

    _____

5. Having bought some candy _____

    _____

6. Having given his friend a hat _____

    _____

7. Having moved to a farm _____

    _____

8. Having heard a siren _____

    _____

9. Having dropped an ice cream cone _____

    _____

10. Having brushed her teeth _____

    _____

11. Having sat on wet paint _____

    _____

144

Name_____   **HAVING + PAST PARTICIPLE**

Date_____

The following is the pattern for writing phrases beginning with "having" and using the past participle.

Pattern: **Having** + past participle + word(s) + a comma + subject + rest of sentence

                                                    comma ↗
Example: **Having** stood on my head, *I* felt dizzy.
                            past   subject
                            participle   rest of sentence

            [phrase   ]

                        ⚷ ⚷ ⚷ ⚷ ⚷

Directions: *Having*, the past participle, and words have been written for you. Place a comma, write a subject, and complete the sentence.

        Example: Having learned her alphabet, **Susie said the**

                    ABC's for the entire class.

1.   Having dropped a dime _____

    _____

2.   Having listened carefully _____

    _____

3.   Having set the box on the table _____

    _____

145

4. Having fixed the car _____

_____

5. Having fallen out of bed _____

_____

6. Having rollerskated for four hours _____

_____

7. Having helped the older man from the car _____

_____

8. Having missed the bus _____

_____

9. Having built a fort _____

_____

10. Having stubbed her toe _____

_____

11. Having called for help _____

_____

146

Name_____   **HAVING + PAST PARTICIPLE**
                                                        CONSTRUCTION
Date_____

As you read, you will note that authors have used phrases beginning with *having* in their writing. Find examples. Write each example and its source (where you found it).

Sentence: _____

_____

Source: _____

Sentence: _____

_____

Source: _____

Sentence: _____

_____

Source: _____

Sentence: _____

_____

Source: _____

Sentence: _____

_____

Source: _____

ŏ ŏ

Sentence: _____

_____

Source: _____

ŏ ŏ

Sentence: _____

_____

Source: _____

ŏ ŏ

Sentence: _____

_____

Source: _____

ŏ ŏ

Sentence: _____

_____

Source: _____

UNIT VII

SUBORDINATE CLAUSES

For effective teaching strategies, please refer to page 14.

A clause has a subject and a verb. The subject tells **who** or **what** a sentence is about.

    Example: A <u>pig</u> lay in the mud.

This sentence is about a *pig. Pig* is the subject.

A verb tells **what is (was)** or **what happens (happened)**.

    Example: A <u>pig</u> <u>lay</u> in the mud.

Lay tells what happened in the sentence. *Lay* is the verb. We place one line under the word, <u>pig</u>, to show it is the subject. We place two lines under the word, <u>lay</u>, to show it is the verb.

A clause has a subject and a verb. The sentence, "*A pig lay in the mud.*" is a clause because it has both a subject and a verb. This clause says a complete thought and is called an **independent clause**.

Another type of clause is a **dependent clause**. It does have a subject and a verb, but it sounds like the person quit talking in the middle of the thought.

    Example: Before <u>I</u> <u>eat</u> dinner

The subject of the clause is *I.* The verb is *eat.* However, we have no idea how the person may finish his thought. We are left not knowing what the person does before

151

he eats dinner. A clause that has a subject and a verb but does not state a complete thought is called a **dependent clause**. It cannot stand alone as a sentence.

You will notice that there are certain words that will begin dependent clauses. For this unit, we will talk about **subordinating conjunctions**. Do not let that term scare you. For our lessons, they are simply words that begin dependent clauses:

after

although

as

because

before

if

since

unless

until

when

whenever

while

Although there are other subordinating conjunctions, these are the easiest to learn and are used often.

ᛞ ᛞ ᛞ ᛞ ᛞ

Directions: Read each clause. Underline the subject once and the verb twice.

    Example: When <u>Carl</u> <u>comes</u> here

1.   The man licked the stamp.

2.   Before you eat dinner

3.   When the lights dimmed

4.   While I ate

5.   Their sister plays on a team.

6.   Because the cat likes me

7.   After Mike washed his car

8.   My dog drank all of his water.

9.   Until Dad leaves

10.   Although my aunt drives

ᔕ ᔕ ᔕ ᔕ ᔕ

Directions: Read each clause carefully.   Check any clause that cannot stand alone as a sentence because it does not say a complete thought. This type of clause is called a **dependent clause**.

1.   ____   The man licked the stamp.

2.   ____   Before you eat dinner.

3.   ____   When the lights dimmed.

4.   ____   While I ate.

5.   ____   Their sister plays on a team.

6.   ____   Because the cat likes me.

7.   ____   After Mike washed his car.

8.   ____   My dog drank all of his water.

9.   ____   Until Dad leaves.

10. ____   Although my aunt drives.

ADDITIONAL WRITING SPACE

A clause has a subject and a verb. The subject tells **who** or **what** a sentence is about.

>   **Example:**   A <u>frog</u> hopped along.

This sentence is about a *frog*. *Frog* is the subject.

A verb tells **what is** (**was**) or **what happens** (**happened**).

>   **Example:**   A <u>frog</u> <u>hopped</u> along.

Hopped tells what happened in the sentence. *Hopped* is the verb. We place one

line under the word, *<u>frog,</u>* to show it is the subject. We place two lines under the word,

hopped, to show it is the verb.

A clause has a subject and a verb. The sentence, "*A frog hopped along,*" is a clause

because it has both a subject and a verb. This clause says a complete thought and is

called an **independent clause**.

Another type of clause is a **dependent clause**. It does have a subject and a verb,

but it sounds like the person quit talking in the middle of the thought.

>   **Example:**   When <u>she</u> <u>goes</u> home

The subject of the clause is *she*. The verb is *goes*. However, we have no idea how

the person may finish the thought. We are left not knowing what the person is going to say about what the lady does when she goes home. A clause that has a subject and a verb but does not state a complete thought is called a **dependent clause**. It is not a complete sentence.

You will notice that there are certain words that will begin dependent clauses. For this unit, we will talk about **subordinating conjunctions**. Do not let that term scare you; for our lessons, they are simply words that begin dependent clauses:

after	**since**
although	**unless**
as	**until**
because	**when**
before	**whenever**
if	**while**

Although there are other subordinating conjunctions, these are the easiest to learn and are used often.

🜲 🜲 🜲 🜲 🜲

Directions: Read each clause. Underline the subject once and the verb twice.

   Example: Because I dive

1.   A ball rolled across the lawn.

2.   Henry likes this shell.

3.   If it snows

4.   Those boys are friends.

5.   Before we leave

6.   Our yard is very small.

7.   When ice melts

8.   This bow is bright green.

9.   After Dennis brushes his teeth

10.   That horse likes to run.

🫐 🫐 🫐 🫐 🫐

Directions: Read each clause carefully. Check any clause that cannot stand alone as a sentence because it does not say a complete thought. This type of clause is called a **dependent clause**.

1.   ____   A ball rolled across the lawn.

2.   ____   Henry likes this shell.

3.   ____   If it snows.

4.   ____   Those boys are friends.

5.   ____   Before we leave.

6.   ____   Our yard is very small.

7.   ____   When ice melts.

8.   ____   This bow is bright green.

9.   ____   After Dennis brushes his teeth.

10.   ____   That horse likes to run.

Name_____

Date_____

INDEPENDENT CLAUSES
and DEPENDENT CLAUSES

A clause always contains a subject and a verb.

    A.   An **independent clause** can stand alone as a complete thought.

    B.   A **dependent clause** cannot stand alone as a sentence.

        1.   It does not say a complete thought.

        2.   It sounds like someone forgot to finish the sentence.

           Ĭ Ĭ Ĭ Ĭ Ĭ

Directions: Read each clause carefully. Check any clause that cannot stand alone as a sentence because it does not say a complete thought. This type of clause is called a **dependent clause**.

1. _____   When Tim laughs.

2. _____   When Tim laughs, tears roll down his cheeks.

3. _____   If you want to sing.

4. _____   I'll sing if you want to sing.

5. _____   Because she could not go.

6. _____   Because her mom works, she could not go.

7. _____   The boys ate after they played football.

8. _____   We like to read.

9. _____   Before we read.

A clause always contains a subject and a verb.

An **independent clause** can stand alone as a complete thought.

A **dependent clause** does not say a complete thought and cannot stand alone as a sentence.

       Example: Grandma likes to golf.   **(independent clause)**

                      If your grandma golfs   **(dependent clause)**

Directions: If the group of words says a complete thought and can stand alone as a sentence, write **IC** (independent clause) in the blank. If the group of words does not say a complete thought, write **DC** (dependent clause) in the blank.

1.   _____   When this ice melts.

2.   _____   Those boys are friends.

3.   _____   If it rains.

4.   _____   On the table is a small basket.

5.   _____   Although Jenny is hungry.

6.   _____   Before the dog barked.

7.   _____   Because Jim likes to eat.

8.   _____   Our friends live in Texas.

A clause always contains a subject and a verb.

An **independent clause** can stand alone as a complete thought.

A **dependent clause** does not say a complete thought and cannot stand alone as a sentence.

Example: The train left on time.   **(independent clause)**

When the train left   **(dependent clause)**

ぐ ぐ ぐ ぐ ぐ

Directions: If the group of words says a complete thought and can stand alone as a sentence, write **IC** (independent clause) in the blank. If the group of words does not say a complete thought, write **DC** (dependent clause) in the blank.

1. _____   Whenever Dr. Jones speaks.

2. _____   Someone has taken the towel again.

3. _____   Before the music begins.

4. _____   Unless Brad arrives early.

5. _____   If snow falls.

6. _____   After he wrote the note.

7. _____   Her hair was very curly.

8. _____   A stamp is on the floor.

A subordinate clause contains a subject and a verb. It is a type of **dependent clause**. A subordinate clause sounds like someone started to speak and didn't finish the thought.

> **Example:**   After Brad cut the cake

When we write a sentence with a subordinate clause, we start with a word called a **subordinating conjunction** and add a subject and a verb. We place a comma and then finish the thought.

> **Example: After Brad cut the cake,** we ate it.

If we turn the sentence around by placing the subordinate clause at the end, we do not add a comma.

> **Example:**   We ate the cake **after Brad cut it**.

These words are used as subordinating conjunctions: **after, although, as, because, before, if, since, unless, until, when, whenever,** and **while**. There are other subordinating conjunctions, but these are commonly used.

ර් ර් ර් ර් ර්

Directions: Each sentence begins with a subordinating clause. Finish the sentence.

1.   When Tina smiles, she _____

_____

2.   Before Tim leaves, he always _____

_____

3.   If I were you, I would _____

_____

4.   Because Mrs. Samson likes cheese, she _____

_____

5.   Unless my homework is finished, I can't _____

_____

6.   After we went to the store, we _____

_____

7.   Until the bus comes, they _____

_____

8.   Whenever Grandpa comes to visit, he _____

_____

9.   As Sarah was walking to her friend's house, she _____

_____

A subordinate clause contains a subject and a verb. It is a type of **dependent clause**. A subordinate clause sounds like someone started to speak and didn't finish the thought.

> **Example:**   While I was talking

When we write a sentence with a subordinate clause, we start with a word called a **subordinating conjunction** and add a subject and a verb. We place a comma and then finish the thought.

> **Example:**   **While I was talking,** the cat rubbed against my leg.

If we turn the sentence around by placing the subordinate clause at the end, we do not add a comma.

> **Example:**   The cat rubbed against my leg **while I was talking.**

These words are used as subordinating conjunctions: **after, although, as, because, before, if, since, unless, until, when, whenever,** and **while**. There are other subordinating conjunctions, but these are commonly used.

𝄞 𝄞 𝄞 𝄞 𝄞

Directions: Each sentence begins with a subordinating clause. Finish the sentence.

1.   Although his ankle was hurt, the player _____

_____

2. When Marty grows up, he _____

_____

3. If the rain stops soon, let's _____

_____

4. After Gregg and Sue chopped wood, they _____

_____

5. Although Helen is sick, she _____

_____

6. As the play began, Rob _____

_____

7. Unless the team wins the next game, it _____

_____

8. Whenever John sneezes, he _____

_____

9. Because Fred runs fast, he _____

_____

A clause contains a subject and a verb.

> Remember: A subject tells *who* or *what* the sentence is about.
>
> A verb tells *what is* (*was*) or *what happens* (*happened*).
>
> **Example:**   This <u>baby</u> <u>likes</u> me.

The *baby* is who the sentence is about. *Likes* tells what is.

A sentence is a special kind of clause. A sentence is an independent clause. That means it says a complete thought. When someone says or writes a complete thought (independent clause), you understand what is said.

> **Examples:**   My <u>puppy</u> <u>chews</u> paper.
>
> Two <u>eggs</u> <u>fell</u> on the floor.

Sometimes a clause cannot stand alone. It's as if someone started to speak and ran off before finishing. This is called a dependent clause. If a dependent clause begins with one of the following words called **subordinating conjunctions**, the dependent clause is called a subordinate clause.

after	**because**	**since**	**when**
although	**before**	**unless**	**whenever**
as	**if**	**until**	**while**

Remember that there are other words that serve as subordinating conjunctions.

ß ß ß ß ß

Directions: Each sentence begins with a subordinating clause. Finish the sentence.

1.   <u>When the buzzer sounded,</u>_____

_____

2.   After I ate breakfast, _____

    _____

3.   When I was a baby, _____

    _____

4.   Because the toy is broken, _____

    _____

5.   Before we go to bed, _____

    _____

6.   If it rains, _____

    _____

7.   Although I was tired, _____

    _____

8.   Whenever Billy laughs, _____

    _____

9.   Since you finished first, _____

    _____

Name_____ **SUBORDINATE CLAUSES**

Date_____

As you read, you will note that authors have used subordinate clauses in their writing. Find examples. Write each example and its source (where you found it).

Sentence: _____

_____

Source: _____

Sentence: _____

_____

Source: _____

Sentence: _____

_____

Source: _____

Sentence: _____

_____

Source: _____

Sentence: _____

_____

Source: _____

Sentence: _____

_____

Source: _____

Sentence: _____

_____

Source: _____

Sentence: _____

_____

Source: _____

Sentence: _____

_____

Source: _____

168

UNIT VIII

RELATIVE CLAUSES

For effective teaching strategies, please refer to page 14.

For effective teaching strategies, please refer to page 14.

TO THE TEACHER:

1. I have tried to keep "RELATIVE CLAUSES" simple. However, the concept itself is rather complex. You may wish to add that a relative clause may serve as an adjective when it modifies a noun or pronoun in the sentence. A relative clause may also serve as a noun clause when the entire clause serves as a noun.

    Example: The sweater **that is blue and green** was a gift.

    adjective clause
    (modifies sweater)

    Who may go is still being decided.

    noun clause
    (subject of the sentence)

2. Sometimes *that* is omitted from the clause. This is allowed if the meaning of the sentence is not altered.

    Example: This is the pen **that I found.**

    This is the pen **I found.**

3. You may wish to discuss restrictive and nonrestrictive clauses. A **restrictive clause** is essential to the meaning of a sentence and is *not set off by commas.*

    Example: Mr. Price is the man **who gave the speech.**

    restrictive clause

A **nonrestrictive clause** is not essential to the sentence meaning. *Commas are needed to set off nonrestrictive clauses.*

Example: My brother, **who is so funny,** likes to fish.

nonrestrictive clause

At this level, when teaching the unit, I advise you not to determine if the student's written clause is restrictive or nonrestrictive. After the students have mastery of relative clauses, you may choose to go back and teach the concept of restrictive and nonrestrictive clauses. This is an entirely new concept, and many students have difficulty determining if the clause is essential to the sentence.

(I have known English teachers to disagree about restrictive and nonrestrictive clauses. Some clauses are easy to determine; others are difficult or even arguable.)

A clause is a group of words that has a subject and a verb.

The **subject** of a sentence tells *who* or *what* the sentence is about.

> **Example:**   A <u>moose</u> looked at us.

Moose tells what the sentence is about. *Moose* is the subject.

The **verb** tells what *is* (*was*) or what *happens* (*happened*).

> **Example:**   A <u>moose</u> <u>looked</u> at us.

Looked tells what happened. *Looked* is the verb.

🍐 🍐 🍐 🍐 🍐

Directions: Underline the subject once and the verb twice.

> **Example:**   A <u>cow</u> <u>chewed</u> some grass.

1.   Their dad laughed.

2.   Tom goes to school.

3.   A brown horse stood in the barn.

4.   Yesterday, some girls played with dolls.

5.   A loud horn blew.

6.   Jason dropped a cup.

7.   This garden has many weeds.

8.   A friend listens to you.

A clause contains a subject and a verb. A clause may be a complete sentence. That means it says a complete thought. However, a clause does not have to say a complete thought.

Example: After <u>they</u> <u>went</u> to the zoo

They tells who the sentence is about. *They* is the subject. *Went* tells what happened. *Went* is the verb. Although the group of words has both a subject (*they*) and a verb (*went*), we are waiting for more information. We don't know what happened after they went to the zoo. Therefore, "*After they went to the zoo*" is not a complete thought or sentence.

A **relative clause** contains a subject and a verb. It does not stand alone as a sentence. A relative clause may begin with **who**, **whom**, **whose**, **that**, or **which**.

Examples: The woman **who** **came** **to the door** was selling books.
The clerk **whom** <u>**we**</u> <u>**asked**</u> was nice.
That person **whose** <u>**name**</u> <u>**was**</u> <u>**drawn**</u> is very lucky.
I like peanuts **that** <u>**are**</u> **salty**.
Her shoes **which** <u>**are**</u> **new** hurt her feet.

In the examples above, the boldfaced words are called the relative clause. The other words are called the main clause.

Example: *I went to see my uncle* **who is a clown in a circus.**

main clause   **relative clause**

ठ ठ ठ ठ ठ

Directions: The subject of the main clause and a relative clause have been written
            for you. Complete the sentence.

        Example: The club that meets here **will need fifty**

                         extra chairs this week.

1.   The bird that sits on our roof _____

      _____

2.   The apple which rolled under the table _____

      _____

3.   Her cousin who is in the army _____

      _____

4.   A lady whom we saw _____

      _____

5.   The tree that was cut down _____

      _____

6.   A baby whose picture had been taken _____

      _____

7.   The actor who was the star of the show _____

      _____

ADDITIONAL WRITING SPACE

Name_____

Date_____

A clause is a group of words that has a subject and a verb.
The **subject** of a sentence tells *who* or *what* the sentence is about.

> **Example:**   <u>Dad</u> drank chocolate milk.

Dad tells who the sentence is about. *Dad* is the subject.

The **verb** tells what *is* (*was*) or what *happens* (*happened*).

> **Example:**   <u>Dad</u> <u>drank</u> chocolate milk.

Drank tells what happened. *Drank* is the verb.

✄ ✄ ✄ ✄ ✄

Directions: Underline the subject once and the verb twice.

> **Example:**   His <u>son</u> <u>plays</u> soccer.

1.   A child washed several dishes.

2.   My grandma likes ice cream.

3.   That ring is pretty.

4.   They sang loudly.

5.   A large car stopped there.

A clause contains a subject and a verb. A clause may be a complete sentence. That means it says a complete thought. However, a clause does not have to say a complete thought.

> **Example:**   When the <u>teacher</u> <u>talks</u>

Teacher tells who the sentence is about. *Teacher* is the subject. *Talks* tells what happens. *Talks* is the verb. Although the group of words has both a subject (*teacher*) and a verb (*talks*), we are waiting for more information. We don't know what happens when the teacher talks. Therefore, "*When the teacher talks*" is not a complete thought or sentence.

A **relative clause** contains a subject and a verb. It does not stand alone as a sentence. A relative clause may begin with **who**, **whom**, **whose**, **that**, or **which**.

> **Examples:** The girl **who is selling popcorn** is my sister.
>
> The money **that was on the table** belongs to Dan.
>
> That man **whom we saw** was a worker.
>
> Anyone **whose name begins** with ***A*** may leave.
>
> The gift **which I chose** was a large teddy bear.

In the examples above, the boldfaced words are called the relative clause. The other words are called the main clause.

> **Example:** *The child wanted the ball* **that his friend had chosen**.
>
> *main clause*   **relative clause**

Directions: The subject of the main clause and a relative clause have been written for you. Complete the sentence.

> **Example:** <u>The dog that is barking **belongs to the**</u>
>
> <u>**Smith family**</u>.

1. <u>The lady who called my mother</u> _____

   _____

2. <u>The box that is in the corner</u> _____

178

3. Some plants that need more water

4. Her bedroom which is a mess

5. The boy whom we saw at the store

6. Their friend who lives next door to me

7. The boy whose picture won first place

8. The necklace that is silver

9. Linda's aunt who is visiting

10. Games that are long

ADDITIONAL WRITING SPACE

The five words that may be used in relative clauses are: **who**

whom

whose

that

which

There are two important items to remember:

1.   A clause always has a subject and a verb.

2.   An adjective clause will describe something or someone in the sentence.

> **Example:**   Mary is a senior. Mary won the race.
>
> Mary is a senior **who** won the race.
>
> *CLAUSE:*   **who** won the race

𝄞 𝄞 𝄞 𝄞 𝄞

Directions: Combine these sentences using a relative clause.

> **Example:**   That washing machine is dented.
> That washing machine has been reduced in price.
>
> **That washing machine which is dented**
>
> **has been reduced in price.**

1.   Christopher found a suitcase.
     The suitcase had been stolen.   (Use **that.**)

_____

_____

2. The lady just got in line.
   The lady is my mother.   (Use **who.**)

   _____

   _____

3. This poem is the best.
   This poem will be read to the class.   (Use **that.**)

   _____

   _____

4. We have a new friend.
   Our new friend is from Utah.   (Use **who.**)

   _____

   _____

5. The baby's picture was taken.
   The baby is my cousin.   (Use **whose.**)

   _____

   _____

6. The bag is on the table
   The bag contains candy.   (Use **which.**)

   _____

   _____

Name_____   **RELATIVE CLAUSES**

Date_____

The five words that may be used in relative clauses are: **who**

whom

whose

that

which

There are two important items to remember:

1.   A clause always has a subject and a verb.

2.   An adjective clause will describe something or someone in the sentence.

> **Example:**   I need the blue book. The book is on the bottom shelf.
>
>   I need the blue book that is on the bottom shelf.
>
>   *CLAUSE:*   **that is** on the bottom shelf

δ δ δ δ δ

Directions: Combine these sentences using a relative clause.

> **Example:**   I like the new art teacher.
> She replaced Mr. Rend.
>
>   **I like the new art teacher who**
>
>   **replaced Mr. Rend.**

1.   Uncle Bob makes good chicken.
The chicken has been dipped in batter.   (Use **that.**)

_____

_____

2. Dale saw a girl at the store.
   The girl is in his Sunday school class.   (Use **who.**)

   _____

   _____

3. The boys and girls built a snowman.
   The snowman has twigs for arms.   (Use **that.**)

   _____

   _____

4. The boy has black tennis shoes.
   That boy is my brother.   (Use **whose.**)

   _____

   _____

5. Those flowers are on the table.
   Those flowers are from our garden.   (Use **which.**)

   _____

   _____

6. His aunt is a designer.
   She creates unusual opal jewelry.   (Use **who.**)

   _____

   _____

Date_____

A **relative clause** contains a subject and a verb. It is a type of dependent clause

because it cannot stand alone as a complete thought.

> **Example:**   <u>who</u> <u>drew</u> **that picture**
>
> The artist **<u>who</u> <u>drew</u> that picture** has talent.

Note: Sometimes an interrogative sentence may begin with *who*. In this case,
who is the subject of the independent clause.

> **Example:**   <u>Who</u> <u>drew</u> that picture?

In this example, there is no relative clause. *Who* is the subject of the entire sentence.

Directions: Only the subject and relative word have been written. Finish the relative
clause and, then, finish the sentence.

> **Example:**   <u>A small box that **contains marbles and jacks**</u>
>
> **<u>will be given to Ralph as a present.</u>**

1.   <u>I gave the book to Tim who</u>_____

_____

2.   <u>The lake that</u>_____

_____

3. <u>My friend who</u> _____

_____

4. <u>The park which</u> _____

_____

5. <u>The trip that</u> _____

_____

6. <u>The man whose</u> _____

_____

7. <u>I saw a girl who</u> _____

_____

8. <u>The pen that</u> _____

_____

9. <u>I found the keys which</u> _____

_____

A relative clause may begin with **whom**. Often *to*, *for*, or *with* are used in front of **whom**.

Directions: Fill in the blank with whom. Then, read each sentence.

1. Mom asked to _____ I had given the note.

2. Hank wondered with _____ I was going.

186

Name_____   **RELATIVE CLAUSES**

Date_____

A **relative clause** contains a subject and a verb. Because it is a type of dependent

clause, it cannot stand alone as a complete thought.

These words are usually used to start relative clauses: **who**

whom

whose

which

that

𝄞 𝄞 𝄞 𝄞 𝄞

Directions: In sentences 1-10, only the subject and relative word have been written.
Finish the relative clause and, then, finish the sentence.   Sentence 11
has a complete relative clause. Finish that sentence.

Example: The airplane which **landed at gate**

seven is a supersonic jet.

1.   My answer which _____

_____

2.   Frank's aunt who _____

_____

3.   The glasses that _____

4. The shopper whose _____

_____

5. The person who _____

_____

6. A light that _____

_____

7. The player to whom the award was given _____

_____

8. Troy has a grandfather who _____

_____

9. His toy which _____

_____

10. An actor whose _____

_____

11. The plumber for whom Jack works _____

_____

Name_____   **RELATIVE CLAUSES**

Date_____

As you read, you will note that authors have used relative clauses in their writing. Find examples. Write each example and its source (where you found it).

Sentence: _____

_____

Source: _____

Sentence: _____

_____

Source: _____

Sentence: _____

_____

Source: _____

Sentence: _____

_____

Source: _____

Sentence: _____

_____

Source: _____

Sentence: _____

_____

Source: _____

Sentence: _____

_____

Source: _____

Sentence: _____

_____

Source: _____

Sentence: _____

_____

Source: _____

ADDITIONAL WRITING SPACE

IMPORTANT NOTE: As previously stated, you may not need to do every lesson. Monitor and adjust to fit the needs of your students.

UNIT I
ITEMS IN A SERIES
LEVEL 2

EFFECTIVE TEACHING:

The purpose of this book is to teach students how to write more complex sentences. However, do not stop there. Sentences need to come alive, so to speak. Vivid details need to be added to create interest and relay meaning. After students understand a particular pattern, teach them to add words to create interest.

Example: Hannah put on jeans. She tucked them into her boots.

Putting on her **faded gray** jeans, Hannah tucked them **carelessly** into her **paint-splattered hiking** boots.

Be sure to revise using more effective or descriptive words.

Example: *Putting on* her faded gray jeans, Hannah tucked them carelessly into her paint-splattered hiking boots.

Sliding into her **faded gray** jeans, Hannah tucked them **carelessly** into her **paint-splattered hiking** boots.

194

Name_____   **ITEMS IN A SERIES**
                                         Combining Subjects
Date_____

In improving our writing skills, we will combine subjects. One may include more than

two items in a series. Place a comma between each item in a series of three or more.

Place **and** (sometimes **or**) before the last item in a series.

      Example: Her watch is lying on the counter. Her ring is lying on the counter.
                Her bracelet is lying on the counter.

                   Her watch, ring, and bracelet are lying on the counter.

Directions: Combine the subjects of the following sentences.

1. Bricks were used on the patio. Concrete was also used. Tiles were also used on
    the patio.

    _____

    _____

2. Front desk representatives attended the hotel meeting. Valet parking attendants
    went to the hotel meeting. Reservationists attended the hotel meeting.

    _____

    _____

3. Tin cans were scattered in the vacant lot. Broken bottles were scattered in the
    vacant lot. Torn newspapers were scattered in the vacant lot.

    _____

    _____

4. Mike scored well on the math exam. Bobbi Jo scored well on the math exam.
    Tracey scored well on the math exam.

    _____

5. The bank teller seemed uneasy. The loan officer seemed uneasy. The receptionist seemed uneasy.

_____

_____

6. Their television has been repaired. Their radio has been repaired. Their stereo has been repaired, too.

_____

_____

7. Jane's father is a minister. Her brother is also a minister. Her uncle is also a minister.

_____

_____

8. The Carter family is going to the beach. The Gibson family is going to the beach. We are going to the beach.

_____

_____

9. Linguini was featured for lunch. Fettucini was featured for lunch. Lasagna was featured for lunch, also.

_____

_____

10. Small baskets of pink flowers adorned the bridal table. Crepe paper streamers also adorned the bridal table. Satin bows adorned the bridal table, too.

_____

Name_____

Date_____

Often a series will include three or more items.

Example: Chris slid down the waterslide. Kathy and Fred went, too.

__Chris, Kathy, and Fred slid down the waterslide.__

The coordinating conjunctions, **and**, **but**, or **or**, are usually used.

Directions: Combine the subjects of the following sentences.

1. Reference books are in the library. Magazines are in the library. Fiction books can be found there, too.

   _____

   _____

2. Boxes had been piled in the hallway. Luggage had been piled there. Water skis had been piled in the hallway, also.

   _____

   _____

3. Rice will be served for dinner. Noodles may be served instead. Instead of rice or noodles, mashed potatoes may be served.

   _____

   _____

4. Cowboys are riding horses in the rodeo parade. Cowgirls are riding horses in the rodeo parade. Clowns are also riding horses in the rodeo parade.

   _____

   _____

5. John's truck may be used for the trip. Jan's van may be used for the trip. Mindy's station wagon may be used.

   _____

   _____

ADDITIONAL WRITING SPACE

Name_____

Date_____

In learning to improve our writing skills, we will combine subjects of sentences.

Remember that the **subject** of a sentence is **who** or **what** the sentence is about. To

combine subjects, we usually use the coordinating conjunction, **and**. Occasionally,

or will be used. We may use the correlative conjunctions **both...and** by placing

both in front of the first subject.

> **Examples:** The dust pan is under the sink. The whisk broom is under the sink.
>
> A. __The dust pan **and** whisk broom are under the sink.__
>
> B. __**Both** the dust pan **and** whisk broom are under the sink.__

One may also include more than two items in a series. Place a comma between each
item in a series of three or more items; place **and** (sometimes **or**) before the last
item in a series.

> **Example:** Candied apples are good. Baked apples are good. Spiced apples are good.
>
> __Candied apples, baked apples, **and** spiced apples are good.__

ȣ ȣ ȣ ȣ ȣ

Directions: In Part A, join the subjects with **and**.
In Part B, use **both...and** construction.

1. The pitcher hit a ball to right field. The catcher also hit a ball to right field.

A._____

_____

B._____

2. These chopped apples are for your cereal. These bananas are for your cereal.

A. _____

_____

B. _____

_____

3. A wooden duck had been carved by an artist. A totem pole had been carved by the same artist.

A. _____

_____

B. _____

_____

4. That red building will be renovated. The building beside it will also be renovated.

A. _____

_____

B. _____

_____

5. A manicure was given to the salon's client. A pedicure was given to the client.

A. _____

_____

B. _____

_____

When combining subjects, one can use *and*.

> **Example:**   That pillow is ruined. That mattress is ruined, too.
>
>   That pillow **and** mattress are ruined.

One can use *both...and* construction in some sentences. *Both* is placed before the first subject.

> **Example:**   **Both** that pillow **and** mattress are ruined.

Directions: In Part A, join the subjects with *and*.
              In Part B, use *both...and* construction.

1. Crickets hopped through the tall grass. Grasshoppers hopped through the tall grass.

    A._____

    _____

    B._____

    _____

2. A kangaroo is an Australian marsupial. A koala is also an Australian marsupial.

    A._____

    _____

    B._____

    _____

3. Nanette's younger brother plays the piano. Nanette's cousin also plays the piano.

   A. _____

   _____

   B. _____

   _____

4. Corsica is an island east of Italy. Sardinia is an island east of Italy, also.

   A. _____

   _____

   B. _____

   _____

5. A brush is used to groom a horse. A currycomb is also used to groom a horse.

   A. _____

   _____

   B. _____

   _____

6. An egret waded in shallow water. A heron also waded.

   A. _____

   B. _____

   _____

When combining subjects, one can use ***and***.

>   **Example:**   Icicles fell from the Christmas tree. An ornament fell from the Christmas tree.
>
>   _____Icicles **and** an ornament fell from the Christmas tree._____

One can use ***both...and*** construction in some sentences. ***Both*** is placed before the first subject.

>   **Example:**   _____**Both** icicles **and** an ornament fell from the Christmas tree._____

Directions: In Part A, join the subjects with ***and***.
               In Part B, use ***both...and*** construction.

1. Seaweed floated to the shore. A piece of driftwood floated to the shore.

    A._____

    _____

    B._____

    _____

2. Arizona was admitted to the Union in 1912. New Mexico was admitted to the Union in 1912.

    A._____

    _____

    B._____

3. The school play had been written by Steve Platt. The program had also been written by Steve Platt.

A. _____

_____

B. _____

_____

4. Her credit card was lying on the desk. Her keys were lying on the desk, also.

A. _____

_____

B. _____

_____

5. Georgia borders the state of Florida. Alabama also borders the state of Florida.

A. _____

_____

B. _____

_____

When combining subjects, one can use ***and***.

> **Example:** An antique table had been purchased. An antique desk had also been purchased.
>
> __An antique table **and** an antique desk had been purchased.__

One can use ***both...and*** construction in some sentences. ***Both*** is placed before the first subject.

> **Example:** __**Both** an antique *table* **and** an antique desk had been__
> __purchased.__

Another possible construction is the use of ***not only...but also***. ***Not only*** is placed before the first subject

> **Example:** __**Not only** an antique table **but also** an antique desk had__
> __been purchased.__

Directions: In Part A, join the subjects with ***and***.
In Part B, use ***both...and*** construction.
In Part C, use ***not only...but also*** construction.

1. Wind slashed at my face. Sleet also slashed at my face.

   A._____

   B_____

   C._____

2. Cottage cheese had been served for lunch. Peaches had been served, also.

   A._____

B. _____

C. _____

3. Geese are flying south for the winter. Robins are also flying south for the winter.

    A. _____

    B _____

    C. _____

4. This house will be demolished in June. This office building will be demolished in June, too.

    A. _____

    _____

    B. _____

    _____

    C. _____

    _____

5. Ted delivered newspapers last summer. His friend also delivered them.

    A. _____

    B. _____

    C. _____

When combining subjects, one can use *and*.

> **Example:**   A package will be delivered to their home. A registered letter will
> be delivered to their home.
>
> _A package **and** a registered letter will be delivered to their_
> _home._

One can use *both...and* construction in some sentences. Place *both* before the
first subject.

> **Example:**   **Both** a package **and** a registered letter will be delivered to
> their home.

A *not only...but also* construction may also work.

> **Example:**   **Not only** a package **but also** a registered letter will be
> delivered to their home.

ŏ ŏ ŏ ŏ ŏ

Directions: In Part A, join the subjects with *and*.
    In Part B, use *both...and* construction.
    In Part C, use *not only...but also* construction.

1. The judge left the courtroom suddenly. The jury also left the courtroom suddenly.

A._____

_____

B_____

_____

C._____

_____

2. The real estate agent looked at the house. Her clients also looked at the house.

   A. _____

   _____

   B _____

   _____

   C. _____

   _____

3. The Renoir painting was being shown at a museum. A Monet painting was being shown, too.

   A. _____

   _____

   B _____

   _____

   C. _____

   _____

4. The wedding ceremony will be held in the garden of a hotel. The wedding reception will be held there, also.

   A. _____

   _____

   B _____

   _____

   C. _____

Often, items other than subjects can be combined.

> **Example:**   Joe took an algebra test today. Joe also took a chemistry test
>   today.
>
>   _Joe took algebra **and** chemistry tests today._
>
> **Example:**   Miss Smith went to the bank. She also went to the grocery store.
>   She went to the pharmacy, too.
>
>   _Miss Smith went to the bank, to the grocery store, **and** to the_
>
>   _pharmacy today._

When combining three or more items, separate each with a **comma**. Although the
coordinating conjunction, **and**, is usually used in a series, **or** may be used when
appropriate.

> **Example:**   Dick wants to be a doctor. He may want to become a dentist. He
>   may want to be a geologist instead.
>
>   _Dick wants to be a doctor, a dentist, **or** a geologist._

Directions: Combine the sentences by placing items in a series.

1.   The hungry teenager ate popcorn. He also ate pretzels. He ate chips, too.

     _____

     _____

2.   The doctor examined the patient's throat. She examined the patient's ears. She
     also examined the patient's nose.

     _____

     _____

3. Our mechanic placed the pliers into the tool box. He put the jack into the trunk.

_____

_____

4. Her speech should have been longer. Her speech should have been more detailed.

_____

_____

5. A cheerleader yelled loudly for his team. A cheerleader yelled energetically for his team. A cheerleader yelled enthusiastically for his team.

_____

_____

6. Janelle, the errand person, forgot to go to the post office. She forgot to pick up a package at a retail store, also.

_____

_____

7. Josh may leave at noon. He may wait until 2 P. M. Josh may even wait until midnight to leave.

_____

_____

8. Calculators are usually accurate. They are easy to use. They are also convenient.

_____

_____

Often, items other than subjects can be combined.

> **Example:** Margaret raced through a meadow. She reached across a
> stream. She also raced into a barn.
>
> _Margaret raced through a meadow, across a stream, **and** into_
> _a barn._
>
> **Example:** The team may choose a chicken for a mascot. A lizard may be
> chosen. Instead, the team may choose a cougar.
>
> _The team may choose a chicken, a lizard, **or** a cougar for a_
> _mascot._

When combining three or more items, separate each with a **comma**. Although **and**, a
coordinating conjunction, is often used in a series, **or** may be used when appropriate.

Directions: Combine the sentences by placing items in a series.

1. Jeannie enjoys knitting. She also enjoys horseback riding. She enjoys playing
tennis, too.

_____

_____

2. Our neighbor is adventuresome. He is also intelligent. Our neighbor is also
creative.

_____

_____

3. His aunt listened patiently. She also listened sympathetically.

_____

_____

211

4. The family took fishing poles to the lake. The family took a blanket. The family took a camera, too.

   _____

   _____

5. A major corporation decided to hire more employees. It also decided to train a receptionist. The corporation also decided to promote two supervisors.

   _____

   _____

6. The caverns are filled with stalagmites. They also are filled with stalactites. They also contain impressive pools of water.

   _____

   _____

7. Broccoli contains beta carotene. Brussel sprouts contain beta carotene. Carrots contain beta carotene, too.

   _____

   _____

8. The young actress starred in a musical. She starred in a drama. She also starred in a comedy hit.

   _____

   _____

9. The short poem was interesting. The poem was amusing. It was also well-written.

   _____

   _____

The ***both...and*** construction can be used with subjects.

> **Example:**   **Both** the physician **and** her assistant performed the surgery.

The ***both...and*** construction can be used with direct objects.

> **Example:**   Horace received **both** a kit **and** instructions.

The ***both...and*** construction can be used with prepositional phrases.

> **Example:**   Our reference boks have been returned **both** to the public library **and** to the school library.

The ***both...and*** construction can be used in other ways.

> **Examples:**   Her friend is **both** *intelligent* **and** *beautiful*.
>
> *adjectives*
>
> The summary was done **both** *hastily* **and** *inacurrately*.
>
> *adverbs*
>
> Washington, D.C., is **both** a political *center* **and** an economic *hub*.
>
> *predicate nominatives*

Not only... but also construction can also be used and is frequently used for emphasis.

> **Example:**   Washington, D.C., is **not only** a political center **but also** an economic hub.

Directions: Use **both...and** construction in the following sentences.

1. Dalmatians are named for a geographic location. St. Bernards are also named for a geographic location.

   _____

   _____

2. A naval vessel sailed the Atlantic Ocean. A naval vessel sailed the Mediterranean Sea.

   _____

   _____

3. His presentation was expressive. His presentation was also impressive.

   _____

   _____

ă ă ă ă ă

Directions: Use **not only...but also** construction in the following sentences.

1. Wundt was a psychologist. Wundt was also a physiologist.

   _____

   _____

2. Breonna is president of her class. She is drama club president, too.

   _____

   _____

214

The ***both...and*** construction can be used with subjects.

    Example: **Both** rats **and** prairie dogs are rodents.

The ***both...and*** construction can be used with direct objects.

    Example: In Oaxaca, Mexico, **both** Mixtecan **and** Spanish are spoken.

The ***both...and*** construction can be used with predicate nominatives.

    Examples: The special guest is **both** an astronaut **and** a doctor.

                  Lucille Ball was **both** an actress **and** a humanitarian.

The ***both...and*** construction can be used in other ways.

    Examples: The committee's stance was **both** *confusing* **and** *perplexing*.

                                   adjectives

                  That racer is known for driving **both** *carelessly* **and** *fast*.

                                   adverbs

                  The teacher gave **both** *Tina* **and** *Adam* awards for outstanding work.

                        indirect objects

Not only... but also construction can also be used and is frequently used for emphasis.

    Example: Thomas Jefferson **not only** purchased the Louisiana Territory **but also** sent Lewis and Clark to explore it.

215

Directions: Use **both...and** construction in the following sentences.

1.   The postal employee is efficient. The employee is agreeable.

_____

_____

2.   The family went to a museum last Saturday. The family went to an observatory last

Saturday, too.

_____

_____

3.   The youth group presented a religious play. It also presented a concert.

_____

_____

δ δ δ δ δ

Directions: Use **not only...but also** construction in the following sentences.

1.   Peoria is a city in central Illinois. It is also the name of a town in Arizona.

_____

_____

2.   The child screamed loudly. The child threw himself on the floor.

_____

_____

216

Sometimes, items can be joined by *or*.

Example: Jane will attend a football game. Rather than attending the

football game, she may attend a parade.

___Jane will attend a football game **or** a parade.___

Directions: Join the appropriate items in the two sentences with *or*.

1. The lake is oblong. It may be oval.

    _____

2. The caverns are sixty feet below the earth's surface. They may be seventy feet
    below the earth's surface.

    _____

    _____

3. These chairs have been manufactured by Dawson Industries. They may have
    been manufactured by Endel Enterprises.

    _____

    _____

4. Their mother has been in the U. S. Army. She may have been in the Navy.

    _____

5. Mark enjoys mountain climbing on weekends. He sometimes enjoys spelunking
    instead.

    _____

    _____

ADDITIONAL WRITING SPACE

Sometimes, items can be joined by *or*.

> **Example:** Molly Smith, my best friend, wants to become
>
> an actress. She may want to be a biologist.
>
>   Molly Smith, my best friend, wants to become an actress **or**
>
>   a biologist.

Directions: Join the appropriate items in the two sentences with *or*.

1.   The young woman needs to purchase a jacket. She may need to purchase a long coat instead.

    _____

    _____

2.   I may go to the beach next Tuesday. I may go to the mountains instead.

    _____

    _____

3.   Her little brother wants a wagon for his birthday. He might want a tricycle rather than a wagon.

    _____

    _____

4.   The gold watch had been made in Germany. It may have been made in Switzerland.

    _____

    _____

ADDITIONAL WRITING SPACE

Either...or construction can be used with direct objects.

    Example: You must take **either** your *coat* **or** a *sweatshirt*.

Either...or construction can be used with predicate nominatives.

    Example: Jana's middle name is **either** *Marie* **or** *Lee*.

Either...or construction can be used with indirect objects.

    Example: Kay gave **either** *Tom* **or** *Suzanne* some cards.

Either...or construction can be used with prepositional phrases.

    Example: Kelly went **either** *to the zoo* **or** *to a museum*.

Either...or construction can be used with adverbs or adjectives.

    Examples: They **either** went *up* into the attic **or** *down* into the cellar.

                         adverbs

              Her car is **either** *gray* **or** *silver*.

                        adjectives

Either...or construction can be used with verbs.

    Example: He **either** *fell* down some steps **or** *tripped* over a ladder.

Directions: Combine these sentences using ***either...or*** construction.

1.   Janelle's boss gave her a bouquet of tulips as a birthday gift. He may have given her a basket of carnations.

2. Courntey told her aunt a hilarious story. It may have been her uncle to whom she told it.

_____

_____

3. Josh gave his grandmother a necklace. He may have given her a bracelet.

_____

_____

4. Sally Alexander wants to become a computer analyst. She may choose to become an accountant instead.

_____

_____

5. Mrs. Johnson has flown to Miami on a business trip. She may have flown to Chicago, not Miami.

_____

_____

Either...or construction can be used with direct objects.

> **Example:**   Ken usually eats **either** *pizza* **or** a *sandwich* for lunch.

Either...or construction can be used with predicate nominatives.

> **Example:**   The scholarship recipient is **either** *Mark* **or** *Shanna*.

Either...or construction can be used with indirect objects.

> **Example:**   That company sent **either** the *lawyer* **or** her *client* a statement.

Either...or construction can be used with prepositional phrases.

> **Example:**   The annoyed customer spoke **either** *to the manager* **or** *to*
>
> *the owner* of the store.

Either...or construction can be used with adverbs or adjectives.

> **Examples:**   He walks **either** too *slowly* **or** too *fast*.
> *adverbs*
>
> This expedition will be **either** *adventurous* **or** *frightening*.
> *adjectives*

Either...or construction can be used with verbs.

> **Example:**   The crowd **either** *cheered* **or** *heckled* the victorious team.

🍐 🍐 🍐 🍐 🍐

Directions: Combine these sentences using ***either...or*** construction.

1.   Mr. and Mrs. Winters have sent apricots to their former neighbors. They may

have sent oranges rather than apricots.

_____

_____

2. Rebecca has applied for admission to a state university. She may have applied to a community college.

_____

_____

3. Bruce and Robyn want to become physicians. They may wish, instead, to become medical assistants.

_____

_____

4. His manner of speaking can be very pleasant. It can be, at times, extremely churlish.

_____

_____

5. The leader has given the top club member an award. He may have given the top two club members awards.

_____

_____

A. ***Either...or*** can be used to join the subjects of some sentences.

> **Example:** A hermit has come to town.
> It may be the hermit's brother.
>
>   **Either** a hermit **or** his brother has come to town.

When using *either...or* construction, make the verb agree with the subject closer to the verb.

> **Example:** Either the girl or the boys **have** a map.
>
> Either the boys or the girl **has** a map.

B. ***Neither...nor*** can be used to join the subjects of some sentences.

> **Example:** Patty can't ski. Luke can't ski.
>
>   **Neither** Patty **nor** Luke can ski.

When using *neither...nor* construction, make the verb agree with the subject closer to the verb.

> **Example:** Neither this tree nor those flowers **are** to be planted today.
>
> Neither those flowers nor this tree **is** to be planted today.

Directions: Use ***either...or*** or ***neither...nor*** to join subjects of the following sentences.

1. The cargo ship hasn't arrived. The oil tanker hasn't arrived.

   _____

   _____

2. A piece of kelp floated to shore. It may have been a jellyfish that floated to shore.

   _____

   _____

3.　　Clark broke his ankle. It may be the tibia in his leg that is broken.

_____

_____

4.　　The essay winner had not been announced. The science fair winner had not been announced either.

_____

_____

5.　　The photographer will take your picture now. Her assistant may take it.

_____

_____

6.　　Sue is in a hurry. It may be her brothers who are in a hurry.

_____

_____

7.　　William cannot go to the stadium tonight. His cousin cannot go either.

_____

_____

8.　　The boys will be coming to the performance. Their mother may come instead.

_____

_____

9.　　The nurses are not ready for surgery. It may be the doctors who aren't ready.

_____

_____

When joining two complete thoughts, you may use the coordinating conjunctions, **and**, **but**, or **or**.

A.   You must use two **complete** thoughts.

B.   The thoughts (sentences) must be related.

C.   You must place a **comma** before the conjunction.

   Example: The swim team boarded the bus. Victor remained behind.

   The swim team boarded the bus, **but** Victor remained behind.

Directions: Use **and**, **but**, or **or** to combine these sentences.

1.   Swimming is fun. Water skiing is more exciting.

   _____

   _____

2.   Brett will ride the rapids first. His sister will follow.

   _____

   _____

3.   You may take the garbage out now. You may wait until after dinner.

   _____

   _____

4.   Miss Blake was hired for the job. Her first day will be tomorrow.

   _____

   _____

5. An alligator surfaced at the water's edge. It did not come near our canoe.

   _____

   _____

6. Your science report may be written. It may be presented orally.

   _____

   _____

7. The building had been started six months earlier. Rain had slowed construction.

   _____

   _____

8. Mrs. Jones is mayor of that city. Mr. Jones is a councilman.

   _____

   _____

9. Mail was delivered at noon. Her check was not in it.

   _____

   _____

10. The cast iron skillet contained frying bacon. In a kettle, oatmeal bubbled.

    _____

    _____

11. Cindy will earn fifty dollars for her trip. If she doesn't earn fifty dollars, she can't go.

    _____

    _____

When joining two complete thoughts, you may use the coordinating conjunctions, **and**, **but**, or **or**.

    A.   You must use two **complete** thoughts.

    B.   The thoughts (sentences) must be related.

    C.   You must place a **comma** before the conjunction.

       Example: Jan went to a football game. Her sister went out to dinner.

                  <u>Jan went to a football game, **but** her sister went out to dinner.</u>

Directions: Use **and**, **but**, or **or** to combine these sentences.

1.   Megan purchased a camera. She did not buy any film.

_____

_____

2.   Timothy will attend Shippensburg University. He may join the Marine Corps and may not attend Shippensburg University.

_____

_____

3.   Both cockateels and cockatoos are colorful Australian birds. Cockatoos are predominantly white.

_____

_____

4.   Uncle Fred is a financial consultant. Aunt Jane is a journalist.

_____

_____

5. A slight earthquake occurred. It was felt only by a few people.

_____

_____

6. The pinball machine has broken. Dad thinks he can repair it.

_____

_____

7. Mr. Kennedy will move to Atlanta this week. His family will join him after the school year has ended.

_____

_____

8. You may clean the garage today. You may wait until tomorrow.

_____

_____

9. Hannah joined an archaeological dig. She said that it was a thoroughly enjoyable experience.

_____

_____

10. His physician suggested Cecil lose weight. Cecil could be a prime candidate for a heart attack.

_____

_____

Name_____   **ITEMS IN A SERIES**

Date_____

As you read, you will note that authors have used these sentence structures in their writing. Find examples. Write each example and its source.

Sentence: _____

_____

Source: _____

Sentence: _____

_____

Source: _____

Sentence: _____

_____

Source: _____

Sentence: _____

_____

Source: _____

Sentence: _____

_____

Source: _____

🝙 🝙 🝙 🝙 🝙 🝙 🝙 🝙 🝙 🝙 🝙 🝙 🝙 🝙 🝙 🝙 🝙 🝙 🝙 🝙

Sentence: _____

_____

Source: _____

🝙 🝙 🝙 🝙 🝙 🝙 🝙 🝙 🝙 🝙 🝙 🝙 🝙 🝙 🝙 🝙 🝙 🝙 🝙 🝙

Sentence: _____

_____

Source: _____

🝙 🝙 🝙 🝙 🝙 🝙 🝙 🝙 🝙 🝙 🝙 🝙 🝙 🝙 🝙 🝙 🝙 🝙 🝙 🝙

Sentence: _____

_____

Source: _____

🝙 🝙 🝙 🝙 🝙 🝙 🝙 🝙 🝙 🝙 🝙 🝙 🝙 🝙 🝙 🝙 🝙 🝙 🝙 🝙

Sentence: _____

_____

Source: _____

UNIT II

SEMICOLON CONSTRUCTION
Level 2

For effective teaching strategies, please refer to pages 14 and 194.

A semicolon is a comma with a period above it (;). A semicolon joins two thoughts that are about the same topic. The two thoughts joined by a semicolon must be complete thoughts. That means each thought could stand alone as a sentence.

Examples: This painting is an antique,   **(complete thought)**

If dinner isn't ready.   **(not a complete thought)**

(There is a subject [dinner] and a verb [is].

However, we don't know what will happen if dinner isn't ready.)

Lifted weights on Saturday.   **(not a complete thought)**

(We don't know who lifted weights on Saturday. We are missing

a subject.)

George in the afternoon.   **(not a complete thought)**

(We don't know what George did in the afternoon. We are

missing a verb.)

Directions: Write **C** in the blank if the group of words is a complete thought.
Write **NC** if the group of words is not a complete thought.

1. _____   A hot air balloon in the sky.

2. _____   The hose had been left on.

3. _____   Until we meet again.

4. _____ In the middle of the night.

5. _____ Talked with Mr. Franklin about the science test.

6. _____ Building construction has come to a halt.

7. _____ A jewelry box loaded with stones.

8. _____ After the group hiked the canyon.

9. _____ When she is ill.

10. _____ Giving money to charity.

11. _____ The hideout was discovered by the posse.

12. _____ During the early morning, a hobo sat in the park.

13. _____ Lance and Ted's dad a banker.

14. _____ In the corner of the square stands a statue.

15. _____ Although the house is dilapidated.

ꙮ ꙮ ꙮ ꙮ ꙮ

A semicolon may be used to join two complete thoughts about the **same** topic.

Directions: Read the sentences. Place a **+** in the blank if the two thoughts are related. Place a **-** in the blank if they are not related.

1. _____ Sal's voice sounds scratchy; she has laryngitis.

2. _____ The telescope has a special lens; his dad likes to golf.

3. _____ Christmas decorations were opened; ornaments were hung on the holiday tree.

4. _____ The race begins in ten minutes; we need to go to the starting line.

236

A semicolon is used to join two closely related thoughts. Both thoughts must be complete sentences. **And** is not included with a semicolon. The word following a semicolon is not capitalized. Often, words like **therefore**, **however**, and **thus** will follow a semicolon.

> **Example:**   The rodeo will be held this afternoon; our family will attend.
>
> <u>The first show of the rodeo begins at two o'clock; **therefore**,</u>
>
> <u>our family will leave at noon in order to arrive on time.</u>

Note: When using words like **therefore**, **however**, and **thus**, place the semicolon before the word and a comma after it.

Directions: Use a semicolon (;) to join the two sentences. Use **therefore** and **however** in indicated sentences.

1.   Peter plays baseball for the A's. His championship game is today.

_____

_____

2.   Jim's dad is a carpenter. His mom is a real estate agent.

_____

_____

3.   Lunch will be at one o'clock. You may not go out to play.   (Use **therefore**.)

_____

_____

4. Their sister had a tonsillectomy. She was not hospitalized long. (Use *however*.)

_____

_____

5. You must wake tomorrow at 5 A.M. It is wise for you to go to bed early. (Use *therefore*.)

_____

_____

6. His uncle works for a dairy. His aunt stays home with three small children.

_____

_____

7. A large, leafy plant stood in the corner of the room. Beside it was a marble statue of Caesar.

_____

_____

8. The purse was made of fine leather. It has been badly stained. (Use *however*.)

_____

_____

9. That painting is an original Renoir. It is very valuable. (Use *therefore*.)

_____

_____

A semicolon is a comma with a period above it (;). A semicolon joins two thoughts that are about the same topic. The two thoughts joined by a semicolon must be complete thoughts. That means each thought could stand alone as a sentence if we wanted. Do not capitalize the word following a semicolon.

> **Example:** Billy likes chicken. He likes pizza better.
>
> Billy likes chicken; he likes pizza better.

Notice: The thought before the semicolon could stand alone as a sentence. The thought after the semicolon could stand alone as a sentence. Also, both sentences describe what Billy likes to eat. Therefore, we are allowed to use a semicolon to join the complete thoughts into one sentence.

Sometimes, we use **however, therefore,** and other connecting words after the semicolon. When we use one of these connecting words after a semicolon, we must place a comma (,) after the connecting word.

> **Example:** Billy likes chicken; **however,** he likes pizza better.

Directions: The first complete thought has been written for you. Add a semicolon at the end of the complete thought. Add your own complete thought about the same topic after the word **however** or **therefore**. (Do not forget to place a comma after **however** or **therefore**.)

1. She burned her little finger **however** _____

_____

2.   The clown made funny faces **therefore** _____

_____

3.   Millie was hungry **therefore** _____

_____

4.   The kitten chased a butterfly **however** _____

_____

5.   Toby hit the ball to first base **however** _____

_____

6.   He cut his finger **therefore** _____

_____

7.   They ran out of gas **therefore** _____

_____

8.   A glass fell on the floor **however** _____

_____

9.   Gregg rides his bike to school **therefore** _____

_____

Name_____   **SEMICOLON**
CONSTRUCTION

Date_____

The first complete thought has been written. Place a semicolon (;) and write another

complete thought about the same topic.

       Example: <u>This bread is stale**; we need a fresh loaf.**   </u>

1.   <u>A sailboat glided swiftly by   </u>

     <u>   </u>

2.   <u>A frown covered his face   </u>

     <u>   </u>

3.   <u>Janelle swims nearly every day   </u>

     <u>   </u>

4.   <u>The table is piled high with food   </u>

     <u>   </u>

5.   <u>Construction has begun on the home   </u>

     <u>   </u>

6.   <u>The car was badly damaged   </u>

     <u>   </u>

ADDITIONAL WRITING SPACE

A semicolon (;) joins two related thoughts about a similar topic. These thoughts always must be expressed in complete sentences.

Example: The car skidded on a patch of ice. The driver reacted quickly to regain control.

The car skidded on a patch of ice; the driver reacted quickly

to regain control.

When appropriate, connecting words such as *however* and *therefore* may be used.

Example: The car skidded on a patch of ice; **however,** the driver

reacted quickly to regain control.

A comma is placed after these connecting adverbs. Besides *however* and *therefore*, one may use *thus*, *hence*, *consequently*, *thereafter*, and other appropriate adverbs. It is important to remember that the connecting adverb is placed <u>after</u> the semicolon, and a comma is placed <u>after</u> the connecting adverb.

🍐 🍐 🍐 🍐 🍐

Directions: The first complete thought has been written for you. Add a semicolon at the end of the complete thought. Add your own complete thought about the same topic after the word *however* or *therefore*.

1.   The referee raised both hands **therefore** _____

_____

2.   Karen finished first **therefore** _____

_____

3. The fashion show was a success **however** _____

_____

4. The prospectors searched for gold for three months **however** _____

_____

5. A leak had been found in the water pipe **therefore** _____

_____

6. A championship game will be played today **therefore** _____

_____

7. That horse is the one the Fremont family likes best **however** _____

_____

Directions: Finish the sentences, placing a semicolon after the first complete
            thought. Use a connecting adverb if appropriate.

1. The President of the United States spoke on television _____

_____

2. The building had been badly damaged during a hurricane _____

_____

Name_____

Date_____

A semicolon (;) joins two related thoughts. These thoughts must be expressed completely. In other words, the thoughts could stand alone as individual sentences.

Example: The basketball player shot from the foul line. He missed the basket.

The basketball player shot from the foul line; he missed the basket.

When appropriate, connecting adverbs such as ***however, therefore, hence, thus,*** and ***consequently*** may be used. In the previous example, note that the semicolon ends the first complete thought. When using a connecting adverb, a comma is placed after the adverb.

Directions: The first complete thought has been written for you.
Add a semicolon after it. When appropriate, use a connecting adverb such as ***however*** or ***therefore***.

1.   The carpet cleaning company has finished the task _____

_____

2.   Large, pointed rocks stuck out of the water's surface _____

_____

3.   Kyle's brother just received his driver's license _____

_____

4. A pile of bricks lay in their front yard _____

    _____

5. The flight from Boston arrived at 2 P. M. _____

    _____

6. A baby crawled through some autumn leaves _____

    _____

7. A cheese and potato casserole had been placed on the table _____

    _____

8. The phone had been disconnected _____

    _____

9. A large tornado was spotted in the area _____

    _____

10. A new restaurant will open next Tuesday _____

    _____

ACTIVITY: Write your own sentence using a semicolon.

_____

246

Name_____

Date_____

As you read, you will note that authors have used semicolons in their writing. Find examples. Write each example and its source.

Sentence: _____

_____

Source: _____

Sentence: _____

_____

Source: _____

Sentence: _____

_____

Source: _____

Sentence: _____

_____

Source: _____

Sentence: _____

_____

Source: _____

🪙 🪙

Sentence: _____

_____

Source: _____

🪙 🪙

Sentence: _____

_____

Source: _____

🪙 🪙

Sentence: _____

_____

Source: _____

🪙 🪙

Sentence: _____

_____

Source: _____

248

UNIT III

APPOSITIVES
Level 2

For effective teaching strategies, please refer to pages 14 and 194.

A.   An appositive is a group of words that explains something in a sentence.

B.   An appositive is placed by the word it explains.

C.   An appositive is set off by commas. A one-word appositive may be written with or without commas.

Examples: My sister, <u>the girl in the red dress</u>, is a clerk.

His friend, <u>Miss Nina Musser</u>, will come.

The horse, <u>Flavor</u>, won the race.
The horse <u>Flavor</u> won the race.

Directions: Place the appositive beside the word it explains.

Example: The mayor is Mandy Reily. The mayor is cutting the ribbon for the opening of the shopping center.

<u>The mayor, Mandy Reily, is cutting the ribbon for the opening of</u>

<u>the shopping center.</u>

1.   The director is Tom Lang. Tom Lang is head of the Movie Institute.

_____

_____

2.   My aunt is Lydia C. Cameron. My aunt flew to Tahiti.

_____

_____

3.   My brother is Mark. Mark is on the basketball team.

_____

_____

4.   Janelle is my cousin. Janelle is wearing a blue dress.

_____

_____

5.   That ring is an emerald one. That ring is my grandmother's.

_____

_____

6.   Maria is a good athlete. She likes soccer best.

_____

_____

7.   This doll is an antique. It is over one hundred years old.

_____

_____

A.   An appositive is a group of words that explains something in a sentence.

B.   An appositive is placed by the word it explains.

C.   An appositive is set off by commas. A one-word appositive may be written with or without commas.

   Example: Randy's job was collecting tickets at basketball games. His job was fun.

   Randy's job, collecting tickets at basketball games, was fun.

ᵟ ᵟ ᵟ ᵟ ᵟ

Directions: Place the appositive beside the word it explains.

1.   John Davis is president of Diet Enterprises. John Davis presents seminars about weight loss.

   _____

   _____

2.   A cobra is a poisonous snake. A cobra lives in Asia or Africa.

   _____

   _____

3.   Daniel Boone was a famous frontiersman. Daniel Boone blazed the trail into Kentucky.

   _____

   _____

4.   Eagerly Janet read the note. The note was an invitation to a party.

   _____

   _____

5.   A history exam will be given Monday. The history exam is the one all
     Blake High School students dread.

   _____

   _____

6.   Martin's brother is the recipient of a scholarship. Martin's brother will attend
     a nearby university.

   _____

   _____

7.   Professor Daines wrote three children's books. All three were award winners.

   _____

   _____

8.   Peggy is an outstanding cheerleader. Peggy won the state championship for
     cheering.

   _____

   _____

Name_____

Date_____

A. An appositive is a group of words that explains something in a sentence.

B. An appositive is placed by the word it explains.

C. An appositive is set off by commas. A one-word appositive may be written with or without commas.

Examples: My sister, <u>the girl with a baton</u>, is a twirler.

I like this pie, <u>the meringue-topped one</u>.

My friend, <u>Marty</u>, is a singer.

My friend <u>Marty</u> is a singer.

Marty, <u>my friend</u>, is a singer.

Directions: Place the appositive beside the word it explains.

Example: The intruder was a tall man. The intruder wore a costume.

<u>The intruder, a tall man, wore a costume.</u>

1. Ms. Johnson is the director of a women's organization. Ms. Johnson planned a fashion show.

_____

_____

2. The keys fell into the pit. The pit is a hole twenty feet deep.

_____

_____

3. The thoroughbred was the winner of the race. The thoroughbred is owned by the Wilson Family.

_____

_____

4.   Her hair is a mass of curls. Her hair needs to be trimmed.

_____

_____

5.   Sam Jones made two touchdowns during last night's game. Sam Jones is my neighbor.

_____

_____

6.   Vincent Van Gogh was a famous artist. Van Gogh was a friend of Claude Monet.

_____

_____

7.   Please give this to my brother. He is the one holding two balloons.

_____

_____

8.   Mom brought flowers for the pot. The flowers are petunias and daisies.

_____

_____

Name_____

Date_____

A. An appositive is a group of words that explains something in a sentence.

B. An appositive is placed by the word it explains.

C. An appositive is set off by commas. A one-word appositive may be written with or without commas.

Example: The books are on the floor. The books are a reference manual and a telephone directory.

The books, a reference manual and a telephone directory, are on the floor.

δ δ δ δ δ

Directions: Place the appositive beside the word it explains.

1. Jane's dad is a dentist. Jane's dad talked to us about dental care.

_____

_____

2. A Christmas tree was decorated with red lights and silver tinsel. The Christmas tree was a six-foot pine.

_____

_____

3. Please hand me that magazine. It is the one with the President's picture on the front.

_____

_____

4. The house was a run-down shack. The house was over eighty years old.

_____

_____

5. Nick Gillette is an apprentice carpenter. Nick works for his uncle's construction company.

_____

_____

6. Her hair was twisted in a multi-level braid. This was a new style.

_____

_____

7. The Strait of Gibraltar is an opening into the Mediterranean Sea. The Strait of Gibraltar is approximately thirty-five miles long.

_____

_____

8. Mr. Jones arrived with Lucy Morrow. Lucy is the town librarian.

_____

_____

As you read, you will note that authors have used appositives in their writing. Find examples. Write each example and its source.

Sentence: _____

_____

Source: _____

Sentence: _____

_____

Source: _____

Sentence: _____

_____

Source: _____

Sentence: _____

_____

Source: _____

Sentence: _____

_____

Source: _____

ૡ ૡ

Sentence: _____

_____

Source: _____

ૡ ૡ

Sentence: _____

_____

Source: _____

ૡ ૡ

Sentence: _____

_____

Source: _____

ૡ ૡ

Sentence: _____

_____

Source: _____

UNIT IV

PARTICIPIAL PHRASES:
PRESENT PARTICIPLE CONSTRUCTION
Level 2

For effective teaching strategies, please refer to pages 14 and 194.

Introductory participial phrases have three criteria:

    A.   They must be placed at the beginning of a sentence.

    B.   An "ing" verb will be the first word.

    C.   The "ing" verb must have at least one other word with it so that it can be classified as a phrase.

A verb with the <u>ing</u> ending is called a present participle.

    Examples: to kick   =   <u>kicking</u>

                    to yell   =   <u>yelling</u>

                    to run   =   <u>running</u>

A participial phrase   =   **present participle**   +   **word(s)**

    Examples: kicking a football

                    yelling at the intruder

Directions: Write the present participle of the following verbs:

1.   to laugh -_____

2.   to chase -_____

3.   to lift -_____

4.   to give -_____

5.   to stay -_____

6.   to go -_____

7.   to believe -_____

Directions: Add a word or group of words to the present participle:

1.   <u>laughing</u>_____

2. __talking__ _____

3. __walking__ _____

4. __leaving__ _____

5. __exploring__ _____

6. __designing__ _____

When a participial phrase is placed at the beginning of a sentence, it is followed by a comma (,), and the subject of the sentence. Any remaining information is placed after the subject.

Example: __Exploring a cave, the spelunkers flashed their lights on pools of clear water.__

ᕮ ᕮ ᕮ ᕮ ᕮ

Directions: The participial phrase has been written for you. Write a comma, the subject, and the rest of the sentence.

1. __Stopping suddenly__ _____

_____

2. __Dribbling a basketball__ _____

_____

3. __Climbing down the steep mountain__ _____

_____

4. __Playing a game__ _____

Introductory participial phrases have three criteria:

    A.   They must be placed at the beginning of a sentence.

    B.   An "ing" verb will be the first word.

    C.   The "ing" verb must have at least one other word with it so that it can be classified as a phrase.

A verb with the <u>ing</u> ending is called a present participle.

    Examples: to find   =   <u>finding</u>

                    to swim   =   <u>swimming</u>

                    to see   =   <u>seeing</u>

A participial phrase   =   present participle + word(s)

    Examples: finding a treasure chest

                    swimming five laps

                    seeing his friend

Directions: Write the present participle of the following verbs:

1.   to drive -_____

2.   to hit -_____

3.   to play -_____

4.   to finish -_____

5.   to throw -_____

6.   to send -_____

7.   to live -_____

Directions: Add a word or group of words to the present participle:

1. calling _____

2. chasing _____

3. lifting _____

4. giving _____

5. staying _____

6. going _____

7. believing _____

When a participial phrase is placed at the beginning of a sentence, it is followed by a comma (,) and the subject of the sentence. Any remaining information is placed after the subject.

> **Example:** **Running** down the street, the **girl** chased her dog.

ᘓ ᘓ ᘓ ᘓ ᘓ

Directions: The participial phrase has been written for you. Write a comma, the subject, and the rest of the sentence.

1. Jumping into the pool _____

_____

2. Standing in line _____

_____

3. Pulling on a rope _____

_____

Date_____

A participial phrase may be formed by combining the present participle of a verb with a word or group of words.

    A.   The present participle is formed by adding <u>ing</u> to the verb.

        Example: start = <u>starting</u>

    B.   A phrase is a group of words.

        Example: <u>starting in March</u>

An introductory participial phrase is placed at the beginning of a sentence. After an introductory participial phrase, place a comma (,), the subject, and the rest of the sentence.

        Example: <u>Starting in March, the store will close</u>

                     <u>at nine o'clock.</u>

Directions: Write new sentences by using introductory participial phrases.

        Example: The dancer bowed at the end of her performance. The dancer smiled brightly.

                <u>Bowing at the end of her performance, the dancer</u>

                <u>smiled brightly.</u>

1.   The twins were making a bed. The twins tucked in the sheets.

_____

_____

2. The dog was sniffing the floor. The dog searched for food.

    _____

    _____

3. The chef is preparing a salad. The chef added ripe tomatoes.

    _____

    _____

4. Some children are playing in the sand. They are making a sand castle.

    _____

    _____

5. The boat was sailing on rough waters. The boat suddenly capsized.

    _____

    _____

6. Jamie makes faces at her little brother. Jamie tries to scare her little brother.

    _____

    _____

A participial phrase may be formed by combining the present participle of a verb

with a word or group of words.

A.   The present participle is formed by adding <u>ing</u> to the verb.

Example: to slip   =   _slipping_

B.   A phrase is a group of words.

Example: _slipping on an icy step_

An introductory participial phrase is placed at the beginning of a sentence. **After**

an introductory participial phrase, place a comma (,), **the subject, and the**

rest of the sentence.

Example: Riding on a roller coaster, Jody screamed
                with delight.

ᔆ ᔆ ᔆ ᔆ ᔆ

Directions: Write new sentences by using an introductory participial phrase.

Example: The boys were wading in the creek. The boys found an old,
                soggy shoe.

                Wading in the creek, the boys found an old, soggy shoe.

1.   The girl was running down the hall. The girl tripped on her shoelace.

    _____

    _____

2.   Her dad was watching television. Her dad ate popcorn.

_____

_____

3.   The lady was standing in line. The lady read a book.

_____

_____

4.   Jenny is bathing her dog. Jenny rubs shampoo on the dog's fur.

_____

_____

5.   Dad is frying chicken. Dad is getting ready for a picnic.

_____

_____

6.   The little girl threw a tantrum. She stuck her tongue out at us.

_____

_____

Introductory participial phrases have three criteria:

    A.   They must be placed at the beginning of a sentence.

    B.   An "ing" verb will be the first word.

    C.   The "ing" verb must have at least one other word with it so that it can be classified as a phrase.

A verb with the <u>ing</u> ending is called a present participle.

    Examples: to grow   =   <u>growing</u>

                  to sigh   =   <u>sighing</u>

A participial phrase   =   **present participle**   +   **word(s)**

    Examples: growing five inches

                  sighing softly

Directions: A participial phrase has been written for you. Write a comma, the subject, and the rest of the sentence.

1.   <u>Serving the volleyball</u> _____

_____

2.   <u>Baking a cake</u> _____

_____

3.   <u>Singing very loudly</u> _____

_____

4.   Repairing his bike _____

_____

5.   Jumping up and down _____

_____

6.   Tripping over a toy _____

_____

7.   Declaring her innocence _____

_____

8.   Preparing for a hurricane _____

_____

9.   Finding someone's lost puppy _____

_____

10.   Scolding their little brother _____

_____

11.   Pushing a shopping cart _____

_____

Introductory participial phrases have three criteria:

A.   They must be placed at the beginning of a sentence.

B.   An "ing" verb will be the first word.

C.   The "ing" verb must have at least one other word with it so that it can be classified as a phrase.

A verb with the <u>ing</u> ending is called a present participle.

Examples: to fly   =   <u>flying</u>

                 to ask   =   <u>asking</u>

A participial phrase   =   present participle   +   word(s)

Examples: flying in a large airplane

                 asking for help

Pattern: present participle + comma + subject + rest of sentence

Example: <u>Asking for help, the **student** showed the teacher his paper.</u>

Because the participial phrase describes the noun (subject), it can also be called an adjectival phrase.

Directions: A participial phrase has been written for you. Write a comma, the subject, and the rest of the sentence.

1.   <u>Waiting for a bus</u>_____

_____

2.   Drawing a funny picture _____

_____

3.   Choosing partners _____

_____

4.   Discussing their holiday plans _____

_____

5.   Leaning against the wall _____

_____

6.   Realizing her mistake _____

_____

7.   Standing in front of a mirror _____

_____

8.   Writing a check _____

_____

9.   Walking their dog _____

_____

You can begin the sentence with the subject (**who** or **what** the sentence is about),

add a comma, and then write a participial phrase. The remainder of the sentence

will follow the participial phrase.

> **Examples:**   A <u>customer,</u> **browsing** through some books, read
> several book jackets.
>
> The attorney, **opening** her briefcase, smiled at the judge.

Pattern: subject + comma + participial phrase + comma + rest of

sentence

δ δ δ δ δ

Directions: Place a participial phrase after the subject.

> **Example:**   Three ducks waddled down the narrow path. They headed
> toward a barn.
>
> <u>Three ducks, waddling down the narrow path, headed</u>
>
> <u>toward a barn.</u>

1.   The huge castle stands against the side of a mountain. The castle is
five hundred years old.

_____

_____

2. Five cheerleaders yelled loudly. They led their team onto the field.

_____

_____

3. The cat is sleeping peacefully by the fire. He startled the lady who nearly sat on him.

_____

_____

4. A rooster stood in a small, fenced garden. The rooster crowed loudly.

_____

_____

5. The hair stylist cuts hair all day. The hair stylist often stops to answer the phone.

_____

_____

6. The boy cleans his room. The boy also listens to the radio.

_____

_____

276

You can begin the sentence with the subject (**who** or **what** the sentence is about),

add a comma, and then write a participial phrase. The remainder of the sentence

will follow the participial phrase.

> **Example:**   The model, **posing** for a photographer, smiled and
> waved to us.

Pattern: subject + comma + participial phrase + comma + rest of

sentence

ठ ठ ठ ठ ठ

Directions: Place a participial phrase after the subject.

> **Example:**   The wildcat was growling at us. The wildcat licked
> his paw.
>
>   The wildcat, growling at us, licked his paws.
>
> **or**
>
>   The wildcat, licking his paw, growled at us.

1.   The player was running down the court. The player passed the ball.

_____

_____

2.   The bee was buzzing around the room. The bee landed on the table.

_____

3.   Her dad was driving very fast. Her dad braked quickly to avoid hitting an animal in the road.

_____

_____

4.   The motorist is looking very sad. She is checking the dent in her new car.

_____

_____

5.   A large boat slid against a rock. The boat overturned.

_____

_____

6.   Sandy looked at the envelope suspiciously. Sandy checked the postmark.

_____

_____

7.   The flag is blowing in the wind. The flag is our club's banner.

_____

_____

A participial phrase used as an adjective can be placed after the noun or pronoun it modifies.

      Example: Her dad, **standing on his head**, looked comical.

Pattern: **subject + comma + participial phrase + comma + rest of**

                                                     sentence

Directions: The subject, comma, and present participle have been written. Add a word or group of words to the present participle, place a comma, and finish the sentence.

      Example: A tiger, lying **in jungle grass, watched me.**

1.   Her sister, laughing _____

_____

2.   A black ant, crawling _____

_____

3.   Her red balloon, floating _____

_____

4.   A pig, eating _____

_____

5. A customer, looking

_____

_____

6. The well-dressed lady, touching

_____

7. The governor, presenting

_____

8. A stallion, prancing

_____

9. Her long hair, falling

_____

10. A little green frog, hopping

_____

11. One lone, quiet man, sitting

_____

12. A large vase of flowers, tilting

_____

Name_____   **PARTICIPIAL PHRASES**

Date_____

A participial phrase used as an adjective can be placed after the noun or pronoun it modifies.

Example: A cow, **chewing its cud**, stood lazily in the lush meadow.

Pattern: subject + comma + participial phrase + comma + rest of

sentence

Directions: Finish each sentence. Include a participial phrase.

1.   A small squirrel _____

_____

2.   His big brother _____

_____

3.   A fawn _____

_____

4.   The minister _____

_____

5.   A tired mother _____

_____

6.   Her favorite uncle _____

_____

7.   A policeman _____

_____

8.   Their pet parakeet _____

_____

9.   A store clerk _____

_____

10.   A small brown snake _____

_____

11.   That tall man _____

_____

12.   The farmer _____

_____

13.   A busy secretary _____

_____

282

A verbal is a word derived from a verb. The present participle form is a verbal.

Example: to pace   =   **pacing**

Sometimes a single *ing* word will appear at the beginning of a sentence. This will be derived from a verb. The same format is used as in the introductory participial phrase.

Example: **Pacing**, he waited for the telephone call.

verbal

Pattern: present participle   +   comma   +   subject   +   rest of sentence

ó ó ó ó ó

Directions: Write an appropriate verbal in the following sentences.

1. _____, the group joined hands.

2. _____, a kitten leaned against my leg.

3. _____, the car's brakes screeched.

4. _____, the basketball player ran down the court.

5. _____, a young mother held her infant.

6. _____, a small monkey looked at the zoo visitors.

7. _____, the teacher handed the student a paper.

ADDITIONAL WRITING SPACE

Name_____   **PARTICIPIAL PHRASES**

Date_____

A verbal is a word derived from a verb. The present participle form is a verbal.

    Example: to blink   =   **blinking**

Sometimes a single *ing* word will appear at the beginning of a sentence. This will be derived from a verb. The same format is used as in the introductory participial phrase.

    Example: <u>**Blinking**, she fought back tears.</u>

              verbal

Pattern: **present participle + comma + subject + rest of sentence**

Directions: Write an appropriate verbal in the following sentences.

1. _____, the upset mother scolded the child.

2. _____, her cheeks grew red.

3. _____, a fellow handed the stranger a box.

4. _____, the man rushed into the warm cottage.

5. _____, the team left the field.

6. _____, a toddler nodded his head.

7. _____, I put on a sweater.

8. _____, they shook hands.

ADDITIONAL WRITING SPACE

A verbal is a word derived from a verb. The present participle form is a verbal.

   Example: to choke = **choking**

Sometimes a single *ing* word will appear at the beginning of a sentence. This will be derived from a verb. The same format is used as in the introductory participial phrase.

   Example: <u>**Choking**, the diner lunged across the back of a chair.</u>

         verbal

Pattern: **present participle + comma + subject + rest of sentence**

Directions: Complete each sentence. Place a comma after the verbal. Then, write the subject and the remainder of the sentence.

1. <u>Frowning</u>_____

2. <u>Resting</u>_____

3. <u>Barking</u>_____

4. <u>Laughing</u>_____

5. <u>Running</u>_____

6. <u>Coughing</u>_____

7. <u>Falling</u>_____

ADDITIONAL WRITING SPACE

A verbal is a word derived from a verb. The present participle form is a verbal.

    Example: to search = **searching**

Sometimes a single *ing* word will appear at the beginning of a sentence. This will be derived from a verb. The same format is used as in the introductory participial phrase.

    Example: **Searching**, we found the missing book.
                verbal

Pattern: **present participle + comma + subject + rest of sentence**

                      🍐 🍐 🍐 🍐 🍐

Directions: Complete each sentence. Place a comma after the verbal. Then, write the subject and the remainder of the sentence.

    Example: Laughing, **Mrs. Sims cuddled her baby.**

1.   Yawning _____

2.   Standing _____

3.   Crying _____

4.   Stopping _____

5.   Listening _____

6.   Smiling _____

7.   Limping _____

ADDITIONAL WRITING SPACE

A gerund is another *ing* word. It is, therefore, a verbal.

A gerund is formed by adding *ing* to the verb form. However, a gerund serves as a **noun** in a sentence.

> **Example:**   to fish   =   fishing

Note that a gerund is formed the exact way as a present participle or any other verbal. The *ing* verb form becomes a gerund when it is used as a noun in a sentence.

> **Example:**   <u>**Fishing** is my favorite pastime.</u>

In this sentence, *fishing* is a noun serving as the subject of the sentence.

> **Example:**   <u>I like **fishing.**</u>

In this sentence, *fishing* is a noun serving as a direct object. It is the object that I like.

A **gerund phrase** is formed by adding a word or words to the gerund.

> **Example:**   <u>**Fishing for trout** is very challenging.</u>

Directions: For the practice of gerunds and gerund phrases, we shall work with subjects. The pattern then becomes **gerund or gerund phrase + verb + remainder of the sentence.** Complete each sentence.

> **Example:**   <u>Standing **in line can be aggravating.**</u>

1.   <u>Shopping</u>_____

_____

2. Talking on the telephone _____

   _____

3. Skiing _____

   _____

4. Earning an excellent grade in math _____

   _____

5. Running _____

   _____

6. Traveling to a foreign country _____

   _____

7. Riding a bicycle _____

   _____

8. Going to a lake for the day _____

   _____

9. Picking cotton _____

   _____

A gerund, another word beginning with *ing*, is a verbal.

A gerund is formed by adding *ing* to the verb form. However, a gerund serves as a **noun** in a sentence.

> **Example:**   to swim   =   swimming

Note that a gerund is formed the exact way as a present participle or any other verbal. The *ing* verb form becomes a gerund when it is used as a noun in a sentence.

> **Example:**   <u>**Swimming** can be very rigorous.</u>

In this sentence, *swimming* is a noun serving as the subject of the sentence.

> **Example:**   <u>Harvey's favorite activity is **swimming**.</u>

In this sentence, *swimming* is a noun serving as a predicate nominative. It is the noun after the verb which specifies the activity.

A **gerund phrase** is formed by adding a word or words to the gerund.

> **Example:**   <u>**Swimming in the ocean** requires an understanding</u>
>
> <u>of currents.</u>

ᘓ ᘓ ᘓ ᘓ ᘓ

Directions: For the practice of gerunds and gerund phrases, we shall work with subjects. The pattern then becomes **gerund or gerund phrase + verb + remainder of the sentence.** Complete each sentence.

> **Example:**   <u>Practicing karate **is Laura's favorite pastime**.</u>

1.   <u>Playing a sport</u>_____

_____

2.   Doing dishes _____

_____

3.   Sleeping _____

_____

4.   Getting a traffic ticket _____

_____

5.   Washing a car _____

_____

6.   Going on vacation _____

_____

7.   Laughing _____

_____

8.   Taking a test _____

_____

9.   Finding gold _____

_____

Name_____   **PRESENT PARTICIPLE**
                                          CONSTRUCTION
Date_____

As you read, you will note that authors have used present participle construction in their writing. Find examples. Write each example and its source.

Sentence: _____

_____

Source: _____

Sentence: _____

_____

Source: _____

Sentence: _____

_____

Source: _____

Sentence: _____

_____

Source: _____

Sentence: _____

_____

Source: _____

Sentence: _____

_____

Source: _____

Sentence: _____

_____

Source: _____

Sentence: _____

_____

Source: _____

Sentence: _____

_____

Source: _____

296

UNIT V

PARTICIPIAL PHRASES:

PAST PARTICIPLE CONSTRUCTION
Level 2

For effective teaching strategies, please refer to pages 14 and 194.

The past participle is formed by placing a helping verb such as *had* in front of the verb form.

Examples:	Infinitive	Present	Past	Past Participle
	to park	park(s)	parked	(had) **parked**
	to brush	brush(es)	brushed	(had) **brushed**
	to wash	wash(es)	washed	(had) **washed**
	to eat	eat(s)	ate	(had) **eaten**
	to find	find(s)	found	(had) **found**
	to speak	speak(s)	spoke	(had) **spoken**

Directions: Write the past participle of each verb.

Example: (to pretend)   Charlie had ___pretended___ to understand.

1.   (to cook)   Mom and Dad had _____ spaghetti.

2.   (to start)   The car had _____ easily.

3.   (to practice)   That team had _____ for two hours.

4.   (to eat)   Our guest had already _____ dinner.

5.   (to brush)   She has _____ her teeth.

6.   (to buy)   Their dad had _____ popcorn.

7.   (to score)   Donald had _____ the winning run.

8.   (to swim)   Have·you _____ in a race?

9.   (to run)   The soccer team had _____ past
                         the goal posts.

10. (to paste)   A third grader had _____ pictures on
                         his art paper.

11. (to decorate)   A group had _____ for a party.

12. (to finish)   The workers had _____ sanding the
                         floor.

13. (to drive)   His uncle had _____ them to church.

14. (to depart)   The bus has _____.

15. (to give)   A businessman has _____ computers
                         to our school.

16. (to sell)   Have they _____ their house?

17. (to polish)   His new car was _____ carefully.

18. (to agree)   The lawyers had _____ on a plan of
                         action.

19. (to shake)   This mop should have been _____.

20. (to cry)   Because the child wanted a balloon, she had _____
                         relentlessly.

The past participle is part of the verb. It is formed by placing a helping verb (example: had) in front of a designated verb.

The past participle of a **regular verb** (one that adds *ed* to the past) is usually made by placing a helping verb such as *had* in front of the verb + ed.

Examples:	Infinitive	Present	Past	Past Participle
	to kick	kick(s)	kick**ed**	(had) kick**ed**
	to clean	clean(s)	clean**ed**	(had) clean**ed**

The past participle of an **irregular verb** does not follow the *ed* ending. Each irregular verb has its own special past participle form. One needs to learn these forms so that these can be used correctly both in speaking and writing.

Examples:	Infinitive	Present	Past	Past Participle
	to know	know(s)	knew	(had) **known**
	to bring	bring(s)	brought	(had) **brought**

Directions: Write the past participle of each verb.

Example: (to grab) A batter had ____grabbed____ a large bat.

1. (to help) Lauren has _____ us often.

2. (to sing) Have you ever _____ a solo?

3. (to fly) The jet had _____ many hours.

301

4.   (to park)   A taxi driver had _____ at a bus
                        station.

5.   (to call)   Has your friend _____ yet?

6.   (to steal)   The runner had _____ home during
                        the last inning of the baseball game.

7.   (to break)   Unfortunately, both of Karen's garnet necklaces have

                        _____.

8.   (to look)   We had already _____ under the bed
                        for the lost shoe.

9.   (to repair)   Has your grandmother _____ your
                        telescope?

10. (to see)   Their neighbors have _____ the
                        Washington Monument.

11. (to go)   Several artists had _____ to the
                        same school.

12. (to smell)   Someone had _____ burning paper
                        in a nearby storage area.

13. (to drink)   The smiling youngster had _____ all
                        of his milk.

14. (to watch)   A crowd had _____ three
                        paramedics performing their duties.

15. (to choose)   Has Jordan _____ a project for the
                        science fair?

Name_____   **PAST PARTICIPLE**
                                                CONSTRUCTION
Date_____

The past participle form can be used as a describing word, an adjective.

Used in this way, the word is called a verbal.

Examples: to register   =   _(had) **registered**_   A.   a **registered** nurse

              to please   =   _(had) **pleased**_   B.   a **pleased** look

              to lock   =   _(had) **locked**_   C.   a **locked** door

                            🍐 🍐 🍐 🍐 🍐

Directions: Write the past participle form. Then, write that word in the second space.

      Example: (to roast)   ___(had) **roasted**_____

                                  _____**roasted**_____ marshmallows

  1.   (to deliver)   =   ___(had)_____

                            _____ goods

  2.   (to prefer)   =   ___(had)_____

                            _____ customers

  3.   (to cancel)   =   ___(had)_____

                        a _____ check

  4.   (to disappoint) =   ___(had)_____

                        the _____ child

5.   (to waste)   =   ___(had)_____

                                  _____ time

6.   (to frighten)   =   ___(had)_____

                                  a _____ animal

7.   (to digest)   =   ___(had)_____

                                  _____ food

8.   (to relax)   =   ___(had)_____

                                  a _____ person

9.   (to horrify)   =   ___(had)_____

                                  the _____ woman

10. (to demand)   =   ___(had)_____

                                  a _____ bribe

11. (to inherit)   =   ___(had)_____

                                  an _____ estate

12. (to occupy)   =   ___(had)_____

                                  _____ territory

304

The past participle form can be used as a describing word, an adjective.

Used in this way, the word is called a verbal.

Examples:	to choose	=	<u>(had) **chosen**</u>	A.	a **chosen** people
	to relieve	=	<u>(had) **relieved**</u>	B.	a **relieved** sigh
	to force	=	<u>(had) **forced**</u>	C.	a **forced** entry

ୡ ୡ ୡ ୡ ୡ

Directions: Write the past participle form. Then, write that word in the second space.

Example: (to enlarge)   <u>(had) **enlarged**</u>

<u>   **enlarged**   </u> tonsils

1.   (to reject)   =   <u>(had)   </u>

   a _____ offer

2.   (to postpone)   =   <u>(had)   </u>

   a _____ game

3.   (to annoy)   =   <u>(had)   </u>

   an _____ person

4.   (to furnish)   =   <u>(had)   </u>

   a _____ apartment

5.   (to purify)   =   __(had)_____

                              _____ water

6.   (to establish)   =   __(had)_____

                        an _____ company

7.   (to change)   =   __(had)_____

                              _____ behavior

8.   (to forget)   =   __(had)_____

                        a _____ message

9.   (to dim)   =   __(had)_____

                              _____ healights

10. (to announce)   =   __(had)_____

                        the _____ meeting

11. (to screen)   =   __(had)_____

                        a _____ porch

12. (to worry)   =   __(had)_____

                        a _____ mother

A verbal is a verb form used as an adjective. Frequently, it is placed in front of the noun it describes.

      Examples: to block   =   <u>(had) **blocked**</u>   A.   a **blocked** artery

                     to fall   =   <u>(had) **fallen**</u>   B.   a **fallen** limb

The adjective form (verbal) can also be placed before the subject it describes.

      Example: to stun

                A.   a **stunned** reaction

                B.   **Stunned**, the winner hesitantly took the trophy.

Directions: In the first space, write the verbal of each infinitive. Read the next sentence; write the same verbal in front of the subject.

      Example: to concern

                A.   a <u> **concerned** </u> citizen

                B.   <u> **Concerned** </u>, the citizen called the police.

1.   to embarrass

      A.   an _____ person

      B.   _____, Tom's face turned bright red.

2.   to confuse

      A.   a _____ secretary

      B.   _____, the secretary frowned.

3. to determine

    A. a _____ young woman

    B. _____, Joanna pushed harder against the rock.

4. to soften

    A. _____ butter

    B. _____, the butter was ready to be added to the batter.

5. to agitate

    A. an _____ customer

    B. _____, the customer again explained why she didn't want the product.

6. to forget

    A. a _____ watch

    B. _____, the watch lay by the sink for three days.

7. to confuse

    A. a _____ motorist

    B. _____, the motorist exited the freeway.

A verbal is a verb form used as an adjective. Frequently, it is placed in front of the noun it describes.

    Examples: to admire = _(had) **admired**_   A. an **admired** ruler

                      to break = _(had) **broken**_   B. a **broken** toy

The adjective form (verbal) can also be placed before the subject it describes.

    Example: to lose

              A.   **lost** hikers

              B.   **Lost**, the hikers discussed which trail to take.

                            🍐 🍐 🍐 🍐 🍐

Directions: In the first space, write the verbal of each infinitive. Read the next sentence; write the same verbal in front of the subject.

    Example: to tire

              A.   a __**tired**__ worker

              B.   __**Tired**__, the worker lay under an apple tree.

1.   to secure

    A.   a _____ boat

    B.   _____, the boat rocked idly in the water.

2.   to stall

    A.   a _____ vehicle

    B.   _____, the vehicle blocked the intersection.

3. to cherish

    A.   a _____ ring

    B.   _____, the antique ring was kept in a velvet-lined jewelry case.

4. to saturate

    A.   a _____ cloth

    B.   _____, the cloth dripped gravy all over the floor.

5. to restrict

    A.   a _____ area

    B.   _____, the area was off limits to everyone but army personnel.

6. to remodel

    A.   a _____ house

    B.   _____, the house was worth twice its original value.

7. to fascinate

    A.   a _____ toddler

    B.   _____, the toddler watched the fireworks burst across the night sky.

Name_____   **USING THE PAST PARTICIPLE**
                                              AS AN ADJECTIVE
Date_____

The past participle form can be used alone to describe something. The past participle

becomes a special type of adjective called a verbal.

Examples:	Infinitive	Present	Past	Past Participle
	to beat	beat(s)	beat	(had) **beaten**
	to break	break(s)	broke	(had) **broken**
	to exhaust	exhaust(s)	exhausted	(had) **exhausted**

One can use the past participle (verbal) in front of a noun or a pronoun.

> **Examples:**   a **broken** wagon
>
> an **exhausted** child

One can also write the verbal first, add a comma, and then write the subject (noun or

pronoun) and the remainder of the sentence.

> **Examples:**   **Exhausted**, the *climber* pulled on the ropes.
>
> **Beaten**, the silent *team* left the field.

𝄃 𝄃 𝄃 𝄃 𝄃

Directions: A verbal (past participle form) has been written for you. A comma and a
              subject have also been written.   Finish the sentence.

> **Example:**   Refreshed, the jogger **began to sprint**.

1.   Frustrated, the driver _____

_____

2. _Matted, the dog's coat_ _____

_____

3. _Cornered, the frightened raccoon_ _____

_____

4. _Hidden, a camera_ _____

_____

5. _Discouraged, the math teacher_ _____

_____

6. _Freed, a tiny butterfly_ _____

_____

7. _Distracted, Amy and Marcus_ _____

_____

8. _Surprised, she_ _____

_____

9. _Worried, the physician_ _____

_____

Name_____

Date_____

The past participle form can be used alone to describe something. The past participle

becomes a special type of adjective called a verbal.

Examples:	Infinitive	Present	Past	Past Participle
	to trip	trip(s)	tripped	(had) **tripped**
	to close	close(s)	closed	(had) **closed**
	to steal	steal(s)	stole	(had) **stolen**

One can use the past participle (verbal) in front of a noun or a pronoun.

Examples: a **closed** door

a **stolen** bicycle

One can also write the verbal first, add a comma, and then write the subject (noun or

pronoun) and the remainder of the sentence.

Examples: **Tripped**, _she_ stumbled forward aimlessly.

Closed, the restaurant seemed immersed in darkness.

ᕼ ᕼ ᕼ ᕼ ᕼ

Directions: A verbal (past participle form) has been written for you. A comma and a
subject have also been written. Finish the sentence.

Example: Terrified, the woman **screamed and fled**.

1.   Contented, his baby brother _____

_____

2.   Delighted, the young woman _____

_____

3.   Frightened, a small yellow bird _____

_____

4.   Disgusted, the journalist _____

_____

5.   Troubled, Mr. Grange _____

_____

6.   Preoccupied, a young mother _____

_____

7.   Elated, her brother _____

_____

8.   Amazed, the crowd _____

_____

9.   Puzzled, the little boy _____

_____

The past participle is part of the verb made by placing a helping verb in front of it. Usually, the helping verbs are *has*, *have*, or *had*.

Examples:	Infinitive	Present	Past	Past Participle
	to jump	jump(s)	jumped	(had) **jumped**
	to talk	talk(s)	talked	(had) **talked**
	to take	take(s)	took	(had) **taken**
	to drive	drive(s)	drove	(had) **driven**

Begin a sentence with a past participle and then add a word or group of words. Add a comma, the subject, and the remainder of the sentence.

Examples: **Jumped by a masked man**, the guard fell to the ground.

Talked into going, Cheri climbed into the car.

Taken to an emergency room, the teen received treatment.

Driven by a desire to win, the racer sped ahead.

Directions: In each sentence, the participial phrase has been written. Finish each sentence. Be sure to add a comma after the participial phrase.

Example: Hurt by their remark, **she smiled sadly**.

1. Given extra time to do the project _____

_____

2. Disturbed by a large phone bill _____

3.   Placed on top of a shelf

4.   Purchased for a dollar

5.   Lifted from swirling water

6.   Terrified by a loud scream

7.   Discovered by a talent agent

8.   Stranded in the desert

9.   Baked for two hours

The past participle is part of the verb made by placing a helping verb in front of it.

Examples:	Infinitive	Present	Past	Past Participle
	to follow	follow(s)	followed	(had) **followed**
	to cool	cool(s)	cooled	(had) **cooled**
	to go	go(es)	went	(had) **gone**
	to do	do(es)	did	(had) **done**

Begin a sentence with a past participle and add a word or group of words. Add a comma, the subject, and the remainder of the sentence.

Pattern: past participle + word(s) + comma + subject + rest of sentence

This past participial construction can also be referred to as an **adjectival phrase** because it describes a noun or pronoun (the subject of the sentence).

Examples: *Followed by a stray dog*, I darted into a store.

Cooled by an ocean breeze, the sunbather enjoyed her day at the beach.

Gone within seconds, the raindrops evaporated in the rays of the sun.

Done carefully and thoughtfully, his paper received an outstanding grade.

ᦺ ᦺ ᦺ ᦺ ᦺ

Directions: A participial phrase has been written. Place a comma and finish each sentence.

1.   Stained by red ink _____

2. Found in a vacant lot

3. Warmed by a campfire

4. Tired of watching televsion

5. Urged to do their best

6. Written in a hurry

7. Exhausted from a long hike

8. Freed after the Civil War

A participial phrase may be formed by writing the past participle form and adding a word or group of words.

In a regular verb, the past participle adds *ed* to the verb and uses a helping (auxiliary) verb. With irregular verbs, the past participle will follow a set pattern.

Examples:	Infinitive	Present	Past	Past Participle
	to hurry	hurry(ies)	hurried	(had) **hurried**
	to start	start(s)	started	(had) **started**
	to take	take(s)	took	(had) **taken**
	to blow	blow(s)	blew	(had) **blown**

Pattern: past participle   +   word(s)   +   comma   +   subject   +   rest of sentence

This past participial construction can also be referred to as an **adjectival phrase** because it describes a noun or pronoun (the subject of that sentence).

Examples: *Hurried by rapidly falling snow*, Josh rode his bike faster.

Started in 1971, that business has flourished.

Taken to the mall, Carrie shopped for birthday gifts.

Blown up by a little girl, the balloons danced in the spring breeze.

Directions: A participial phrase has been written. Place a comma and finish each sentence.

1.   Stopped by a policeman _____

_____

2.   Stripped of its old paint _____

_____

3.   Written at the last moment _____

_____

4.   Hidden in the shadows _____

_____

5.   Stuffed inside the desk drawer _____

_____

6.   Prepared by a master chef _____

_____

7.   Finished with their chores _____

_____

8.   Decorated with streamers and balloons _____

_____

9.   Ridden at a steady gallop _____

_____

The past participle = helping verb + appropriate verb.

Examples:	Infinitive	Present	Past	Past Participle
	to admire	admire(s)	admired	(had) **admired**
	to seat	seat(s)	seated	(had) **seated**
	to write	write(s)	wrote	(had) **written**
	to speak	speak(s)	spoke	(had) **spoken**

The pattern for past participle construction is somewhat complicated. Begin a sentence with a past participle; add a word or group of words. Place a comma. Add a subject and the remainder of the sentence.

> **Examples:** *Admired for her talent*, she was given a scholarship.
>
> *Seated on a window sill*, the lad read a book.
>
> *Written by her mother*, the note was a reminder to run some errands.
>
> *Spoken in a soft voice*, his words expressed sympathy.

This past participial construction can also be referred to as an adjectival phrase because it describes a noun or pronoun (the subject of the sentence).

ᔕ ᔕ ᔕ ᔕ ᔕ

Directions: A past participle and a word have been written for you. Add a word or words, a comma, and the subject of the sentence. Write the remainder of the thought.

> **Example:** <u>Listed with **XYZ Realty, the house sold quickly**.</u>

1.   <u>Given by</u>_____

_____

2. _Started in_ _____

_____

3. _Found near_ _____

_____

4. _Drawn on_ _____

_____

5. _Purchased for_ _____

_____

6. _Sent by_ _____

_____

7. _Taken to_ _____

_____

8. _Tackled by_ _____

_____

9. _Distracted by_ _____

_____

322

Name_____

Date_____

The past participle = helping verb + appropriate verb.

Examples:	Infinitive	Present	Past	Past Participle
	to begin	begn(s)	began	(had) **begun**
	to find	find(s)	found	(had) **found**
	to tell	tell(s)	told	(had) **told**
	to view	view(s)	viewed	(had) **viewed**

The pattern for past participle construction is somewhat complicated. Begin a sentence with a past participle; add a word or group of words. Place a comma. Add a subject and the remainder of the sentence.

> **Examples:** *Begun as a colony*, Jamestown grew rapidly.
>
> *Found in the desert*, the old wagon was weathered.
>
> *Told to sit down*, Morgan's sister began to cry.
>
> *Viewed from the upper seats*, the basketball game wasn't
>
> very exciting.

This past participial construction can also be referred to as an adjectival phrase because it describes a noun or pronoun (the subject of the sentence).

𝄞 𝄞 𝄞 𝄞 𝄞

Directions: A past participle and a word have been written for you. Add a word or words, a comma, and the subject of the sentence. Write the remainder of the thought.

> **Example:** Dropped on **the floor, the egg broke.**

1. Selected as _____

323

_____

2.   Fastened to _____

_____

3.   Scored by _____

_____

4.   Dissolved in _____

_____

5.   Kept neatly in _____

_____

6.   Returned to _____

_____

7.   Hurled into _____

_____

8.   Teased by _____

_____

9.   Dressed casually in _____

324

_____

Name_____   **PAST PARTICIPLE**
                                 CONSTRUCTION
Date_____

A participial phrase = past participle + word or phrase (group of words).

    Example: **Listed** in good condition

A participial phrase may be placed at the beginning of a sentence.

    Example: *Listed in good condition,* the patient was recuperating well.

A participial phrase may be placed at other places in the sentence.

    Example: The patient, *listed in good condition,* was recuperating well.

Directions: Complete each sentence.

1.   The girl, taken by surprise, _____

    _____

2.   This cup, broken into several pieces, _____

    _____

3.   Their father, given an award by the mayor, _____

    _____

4.   The rose bush, planted in the fall, _____

    _____

5.   The book, dedicated to Mr. and Mrs. Harrison, _____

6.   The Statue of Liberty, restored for our nation's celebration,

_____

7.   The bride, given in marriage by her father,

_____

8.   The telephone bill, received at the end of the month,

_____

9.   His answer, said in a loud voice,

_____

10.   A large bear, disturbed by a loud crash,

_____

11.   The guest, greeted at the door by the hostess,

_____

12.   Ice cream, thawed for an hour,

_____

13.   The cave, discovered recently,

_____

Date_____

A participial phrase = past participle + word or phrase (group of words).

> **Example:** **Produced** by a major network

A participial phrase may be placed at the beginning of a sentence.

> **Example:** *Produced by a major network,* the comedy was a success.

A participial phrase may be placed at other places in the sentence.

> **Example:** The comedy, *produced by a major network,* was a success.

Directions: Complete each sentence.

1. Frank's mother, known for her great cookies, _____

   _____

2. The automobile, stalled in the middle of the street, _____

   _____

3. Mary's party, attended by twenty of her friends, _____

   _____

4. Mr. Pratt, born in Canada, _____

   _____

327

5.   Our neighbor, disguised as an elf, _____

_____

6.   The story, released to the press, _____

_____

7.   Jack's response, whispered to a friend, _____

_____

8.   The last guest, delayed by a snow storm, _____

_____

9.   An egg, protected by a thin shell, _____

_____

10. The antique rocker, inherited from their grandmother, _____

_____

11. The clothing, manufactured in Maine, _____

_____

12. Her idea, presented to the group, _____

_____

Name_____   **PAST PARTICIPLE**
                                      CONSTRUCTION
Date_____

As you read, you will note that authors have used past participle construction in
forming participial phrases in their writing. Find examples. Write each example and its
source.

Sentence: _____

_____

Source: _____

Sentence: _____

_____

Source: _____

Sentence: _____

_____

Source: _____

Sentence: _____

_____

Source: _____

Sentence: _____

_____

Source: _____

ꝺ ꝺ

Sentence: _____

_____

Source: _____

ꝺ ꝺ

Sentence: _____

_____

Source: _____

ꝺ ꝺ

Sentence: _____

_____

Source: _____

ꝺ ꝺ

Sentence: _____

_____

Source: _____

UNIT VI

HAVING + PAST PARTICIPLE CONSTRUCTION

Level 2

For effective teaching strategies, please refer to pages 14 and 194.

Now that you know how to form the past participle, we can learn more sentence

structures. We will write the word ***having*** and then write the past participle form of the

verb.

      Examples: to faint   A.   <u>had fainted</u>   B.   <u>having fainted</u>

                    to go   A.   <u>had gone</u>   B.   <u>having gone</u>

Directions: Write the past participle in the space provided.

1. (to jump)   A. <u>had</u>_____   B. <u>having</u>_____

2. (to wait)   A. <u>had</u>_____   B. <u>having</u>_____

3. (to talk)   A. <u>had</u>_____   B. <u>having</u>_____

4. (to find)   A. <u>had</u>_____   B. <u>having</u>_____

5. (to play)   A. <u>had</u>_____   B. <u>having</u>_____

6. (to ride)   A. <u>had</u>_____   B. <u>having</u>_____

7. (to walk)   A. <u>had</u>_____   B. <u>having</u>_____

8. (to break)   A. <u>had</u>_____   B. <u>having</u>_____

9. (to pick)   A. <u>had</u>_____   B. <u>having</u>_____

10. (to say)   A. <u>had</u>_____   B. <u>having</u>_____

11. (to fall)   A. <u>had</u>_____   B. <u>having</u>_____

ADDITIONAL WRITING SPACE

Name_____

Date_____

Now that you know how to form the past participle, we can learn more sentence

structures. We will write the word **_having_** and then write the past participle form of the

verb.

Examples: to paint   A. <u>had painted</u>   B. <u>having painted</u>

                to ride   A. <u>had ridden</u>   B. <u>having ridden</u>

Directions: Write the past participle in the space provided.

1. (to blame) A. <u>had</u>_____   B. <u>having</u>_____

2. (to read) A. <u>had</u>_____   B. <u>having</u>_____

3. (to give) A. <u>had</u>_____   B. <u>having</u>_____

4. (to eat) A. <u>had</u>_____   B. <u>having</u>_____

5. (to do) A. <u>had</u>_____   B. <u>having</u>_____

6. (to pause) A. <u>had</u>_____   B. <u>having</u>_____

7. (to grab) A. <u>had</u>_____   B. <u>having</u>_____

8. (to lift) A. <u>had</u>_____   B. <u>having</u>_____

9. (to know) A. <u>had</u>_____   B. <u>having</u>_____

10. (to ring) A. <u>had</u>_____   B. <u>having</u>_____

11. (to push) A. <u>had</u>_____   B. <u>having</u>_____

12. (to set) A. <u>had</u>_____   B. <u>having</u>_____

ADDITIONAL WRITING SPACE

One specific type of sentence structure begins with **having** and adds a participial phrase beginning with a past participle.   (**Having** is a present participle because it is a verb ending with **ing**.)

Pattern: having   +   past participle   +   word(s)   +   comma
+   subject   +   remainder of the sentence

Example: **Having** broken a glass, the two girls swept the kitchen.

past   phrase   comma   subject   rest of sentence
participle

ᵟ ᵟ ᵟ ᵟ ᵟ

Directions: Write an appropriate past participle in each sentence.

1.   Having _____ a cake, Samuel watched television.

2.   Having _____ the ball, the dog lay down.

3.   Having _____ around, the bee flew away.

4.   Having _____ her horse, Wendy cleaned the stable.

5.   Having _____ a gift, the man placed his credit card
back into his wallet.

6.   Having _____ the room, Brad smiled smugly, pleased
with himself.

7. Having _____ the lawn, Carol and Dan stopped to rest.

8. Having _____ dinner, they waited for the dessert tray to be brought to them.

9. Having _____ the wood, she brushed large splinters of wood from her jacket.

10. Having _____ his bike, Ted's face was red.

11. Having _____ their dad, Harry and Joan shrieked with joy.

12. Having _____ four miles, they drank from their water bottles.

13. Having _____ in a creek, the children laughed and joked playfully.

14. Having _____ to the store, they bought several greeting cards.

15. Having _____ a computer program, the woman consulted with her boss.

One specific type of sentence structure begins with **having** and adds a participial phrase beginning with a past participle.   (**Having** is a present participle because it is a verb ending with **ing**.)

Pattern: having   +   past participle   +   word(s)   +   comma

+   subject   +   remainder of the sentence

Example: Having baked a cake, the elderly woman frosted it.

                                                    comma
                        past   phrase   subject   rest of sentence
                        participle

ꝏ ꝏ ꝏ ꝏ ꝏ

Directions: Write an appropriate past participle in each sentence.

1.   Having _____ his homework, he went out to play.

2.   Having _____ her opinion, the woman sat down.

3.   Having _____ to Washington, D.C., Troy went to the White House.

4.   Having _____ the car, the teenager smiled.

5.   Having _____ a letter, the secretary resumed her other duties.

6. Having _____ a tree, the boys and girls stood back, pleased with their accomplishment.

7. Having _____ on a weekend outing, Sally had asked Tina to care for her cats.

8. Having _____ some flowers, Ted seemed uneasy.

9. Having _____ her books, Samantha giggled.

10. Having _____ his watch, Mr. Harper rushed out the door.

11. Having _____ the deserted highway, the couple was concerned about reaching their destination safely.

12. Having _____ their performance, the critic smirked.

13. Having _____ on a farm, I know how strenuous plowing fields can be.

14. Having previously _____ Nellie, my recommendation is to be firm.

To write this specific type of sentence structure, begin with the word *having* and place a past participle after it. A word or phrase (more than one word) follows.

> **Example:**   **Having** jumped off a moving wagon
> past   phrase
> participle

You may recognize this as a type of introductory participial phrase because it begins with an *ing* word.

After the *having* phrase, place a comma, the subject, and the remainder of the sentence.

> **Example:**   **Having** jumped off a moving wagon, Jeff twisted his ankle.
> comma
> subject
> rest of sentence

δ δ δ δ δ

Directions: Write an appropriate past participle form in the first blank. After the subject, write the remainder of the sentence.

> **Example:**   Having _____**sung**_____ a solo, the vocalist **joined**
>
> **the other choir members**._____

1.   Having _____ a novel, he _____

_____

2.   Having _____ a motorcycle, the girl _____

3. Having _____ a general, the officer _____

_____

4. Having _____ some flowers, the florist _____

_____

5. Having _____ for a day, the children _____

_____

6. Having _____ some money, they _____

_____

7. Having _____ the case, the attorney _____

_____

8. Having _____ a cast, the doctor _____

_____

9. Having _____ Phillip's reaction, his mother _____

_____

To write this specific type of sentence structure, begin with the word **_having_** and place

a past participle after it. A word or phrase (more than one word) follows.

> **Example:** **Having** written a letter
>   past   phrase
>   participle

You may recognize this as a type of introductory participial phrase because it begins

with an **_ing_** word.

After the **_having_** phrase, place a comma, the subject, and the remainder of the

sentence.

> **Example:** **Having** written a letter, Kayleigh mailed it.
>   comma
>   subject
>   rest of sentence

ð ð ð ð ð

Directions: Write an appropriate past participle form in the first blank. After the
             subject, write the remainder of the sentence.

Example: Having _____**snapped**_____ a picture, she __**hid**__.

1. Having _____ a painting of a dragon, the artist _____

    _____

2. Having _____ her small gift, the exuberant lady _____

    _____

343

3. Having _____ the game well, the golfer _____

   _____

4. Having _____ to be a carpenter, Sam _____

   _____

5. Having _____ to the store, they _____

   _____

6. Having _____ chocolate chip cookies, Cindy _____

   _____

7. Having _____ the new car, their dad _____

   _____

8. Having _____ at me kindly, the teller _____

   _____

9. Having _____ two plays, the couple _____

   _____

10. Having _____ with her parents, Lalita _____

   _____

344

The pattern for this particular sentence structure is somewhat complicated. First, write the present participle *having*. Add a word or phrase and a comma. Then, add the subject and the remainder of the sentence.

Pattern: *Having* + past participle + word or phrase + comma + subject + rest of sentence

ꙮ ꙮ ꙮ ꙮ ꙮ

Directions: *Having*, the past participle, and part of a phrase have been written. Finish the phrase, add a comma, write a subject, and add the remainder of the sentence.

Example: Having gone to **the Orient, Sue brought back a Thai rug.**

1. Having jumped into _____

_____

2. Having waited for _____

_____

3. Having talked to _____

_____

4. Having found a _____

_____

345

5. <u>Having ridden in</u> _____

_____

6. <u>Having walked to</u> _____

_____

7. <u>Having broken a</u> _____

_____

8. <u>Having picked up</u> _____

_____

9. <u>Having placed some</u> _____

_____

10. <u>Having searched for</u> _____

_____

11. <u>Having tired easily</u> _____

_____

12. <u>Having tried to</u> _____

_____

**HAVING + PAST PARTICIPLE
+ PHRASE**

Pattern: *Having* + past participle + word or phrase + comma
+ subject + rest of sentence

Example: *Having* developed some pictures, Marilyn examined them intently.

comma

past participle   phrase   subject   rest of sentence

𝄞 𝄞 𝄞 𝄞 𝄞

Directions: *Having*, the past participle, and a phrase have been written. Place a
comma and finish the sentence. Be sure to write the subject after the
comma.

Example: Having scanned the horizon, **we were sure that our friends**

had gone into a nearby canyon.

1.   Having asked for a raise _____

_____

2.   Having made brownies _____

_____

3.   Having delivered all of the mail _____

_____

4.   Having finished the reading assignment _____

_____

5.   Having painted his bedroom _____

_____

6.   Having placed the infant in a stroller _____

_____

7.   Having discovered America _____

_____

8.   Having stapled the papers together _____

_____

9.   Having prepared the meal _____

_____

10.   Having swum for two hours _____

_____

11.   Having earned five dollars _____

_____

12.   Having refused to talk _____

_____

Name_____

Date_____

Pattern: *Having* + past participle + word or phrase + comma
+ subject + rest of sentence

ð   ð   ð   ð   ð

Directions: After the word, *having*, place a past participle and word or phrase.
Next, place a comma. After the comma, place the subject and the rest of
your thought.

Example: *Having* fallen off his new bike, Lance called for his father.

comma

past participle   phrase   subject   rest of sentence

1.   Having _____

_____

2.   Having _____

_____

3.   Having _____

_____

4.   Having _____

_____

5.   Having _____

_____

6. _Having_ _____

_____

7. _Having_ _____

_____

8. _Having_ _____

_____

9. _Having_ _____

_____

10. _Having_ _____

_____

11. _Having_ _____

_____

12. _Having_ _____

_____

Name_____

Date_____

Pattern: *Having* + past participle + word or phrase + comma
+ subject + rest of sentence

ᶇ ᶇ ᶇ ᶇ ᶇ

Directions: After the word, *having*, place a past participle and word or phrase.
Next, place a comma. After the comma, place the subject and the rest of
your thought.

Example: *Having* washed the tile floor, Mother slipped on it.

comma

past participle   phrase   subject   rest of sentence

1.   Having _____

_____

2.   Having _____

_____

3.   Having _____

_____

4.   Having _____

_____

5.   Having _____

_____

351

6. _Having_ _____

_____

7. _Having_ _____

_____

8. _Having_ _____

_____

9. _Having_ _____

_____

10. _Having_ _____

_____

11. _Having_ _____

_____

12. _Having_ _____

_____

13. _Having_ _____

_____

This specific sentence construction can also be placed after the subject. The pattern

then becomes: subject + comma + having phrase + comma + remainder of sentence.

Example: The <u>plumber</u>, *having* brought in his tools, checked several pipes.

comma		comma	
subject	past	phrase	rest of sentence
	participle		

Directions: The subject, the first comma, and *having* have been written. Finish the
phrase, add a comma, and complete the sentence.

Example: The lady, having **darted into the street without looking,**

was nearly hit by a van.

1. A bus driver, having _____

_____

2. Her favorite aunt, having _____

_____

3. This jacket, having _____

_____

4. Carole and Bart's dad, having _____

_____

5. My friend, having _____

_____

6. That duck, having _____

_____

7. Their dentist, having _____

_____

8. The nice clown, having _____

_____

9. A tiny baby, having _____

_____

10. Mr. and Mrs. Wilson, having _____

_____

11. Three scuba divers, having _____

_____

12. A fawn, having _____

_____

354

**HAVING + PAST PARTICIPLE
+ PHRASE**

This specific sentence construction can also be placed after the subject.

Pattern: subject + comma + *having* phrase + comma + remainder of sentence

Example: The <u>book</u>, *having* lain on the floor for a week, was tattered.

comma		comma
subject	**past** **phrase**	**rest of sentence**
	participle	

δ δ δ δ δ

Directions: The subject, the first comma, and *having* have been written. Finish the
phrase, add a comma, and complete the sentence.

Example: <u>The queen, having **waved to the crowd,**</u>

   <u>**stood silently as the ceremony began.**</u>

1.   <u>The fisherman, having</u> _____

   _____

2.   <u>Jack's foot, having</u> _____

   _____

3.   <u>This old building, having</u> _____

   _____

4. <u>A chocolate bar, having</u> _____

_____

5. <u>The coach, having</u> _____

_____

6. <u>Their Siamese kitten, having</u> _____

_____

7. <u>Jake, having</u> _____

_____

8. <u>A tall, burly waiter, having</u> _____

_____

9. <u>A group of firemen, having</u> _____

_____

10. <u>These towels, having</u> _____

_____

11. <u>Many alligators, having</u> _____

_____

Name_____

Date_____

As you read, you will note that authors have used phrases beginning with *having* in their writing. Find examples. Write each example and its source.

Sentence: _____

_____

Source: _____

Sentence: _____

_____

Source: _____

Sentence: _____

_____

Source: _____

Sentence: _____

_____

Source: _____

Sentence: _____

_____

Source: _____

Sentence: _____

_____

Source: _____

Sentence: _____

_____

Source: _____

Sentence: _____

_____

Source: _____

Sentence: _____

_____

Source: _____

358

UNIT VII

SUBORDINATE CLAUSES

Level 2

For effective teaching strategies, please refer to pages 14 and 194.

Name_____

Date_____

A clause always has a subject and a verb.

Remember: A subject tells **who** or **what** the sentence is about.

A verb tells **what is (was)** or **what happens (happened)**.

Example: The <u>child</u> <u>sneezed</u> three times.
                                subject   verb

A clause that can stand alone as a complete thought is called an **independent clause**. *The child sneezed three times* is an independent clause.

Sometimes a clause cannot stand alone. It's as if someone started to speak and ran off before finishing. This is a **dependent clause**.

Example: After <u>we</u> <u>ate</u>
                          subject verb

This is still a clause because it contains a subject and verb. The subject is *we*; the verb is *ate*.

👜 👜 👜 👜 👜

Directions: Read the following clauses. If the thought can stand alone, write **IC** (independent clause) in the space. If the sentence sounds as if someone didn't finish it, write **DC** (dependent clause).

1. _____   When Jim was little.

2. _____   If you want to play.

3. _____   The ducks are on the pond.

4. _____   After the batter hit the ball.

5. _____ Jill likes to go to the beach.

6. _____ Although it is snowing.

7. _____ Whenever you finish.

8. _____ A chest is in the attic.

9. _____ Because the ship sailed.

10. _____ The family sat in the first row.

11. _____ Before our church group goes to camp.

12. _____ Jim's uncle is an army general.

13. _____ Your shoes are in the closet.

14. _____ When the Franklins purchased their home.

15. _____ In the tiny boat sat a barking dog.

16. _____ A birthday invitation came in the mail.

17. _____ If you read *Where the Red Fern Grows.*

18. _____ Martin is making a stained glass window.

19. _____ If the band marches in the parade.

20. _____ Their grandmother lives on Elm Street.

Name_____

Date_____

A clause always has a subject and a verb.

   Remember: A subject tells **who** or **what** the sentence is about.

                  A verb tells **what is (was)** or **what happens (happened)**.

        Example: The <u>games</u> <u>are</u> in that cabinet.
                            subject   verb

A clause that can stand alone as a complete thought is called an **independent clause**. The above example is an independent clause.

Sometimes a clause cannot stand alone. It's as if someone started to speak and ran off before finishing. This is a **dependent clause**. A dependent clause can also be called a **subordinate clause**.

        Example: Although the <u>diver</u> <u>surfaced</u> quickly
                            subject   verb

This is still a clause because it contains a subject and verb.

Directions: Read the following clauses. If the thought can stand alone, write **IC** (independent clause) in the space. If the sentence sounds as if someone didn't finish it, write **DC** (dependent clause).

1.   _____   A carnival was held to raise money for the club.

2.   _____   This turtle moves slowly.

3.   _____   Although the pictures have been developed.

4. _____ Before Shirley could utter a word.

5. _____ Her reaction to the problem stunned everyone.

6. _____ I used glue to repair the model airplane.

7. _____ Before you eat dinner.

8. _____ When the lights went out.

9. _____ Unless you are planning to stay.

10. _____ Jonas passed the test.

11. _____ If the tulip bulbs are planted in the autumn.

12. _____ A porcelain vase lay in pieces on the floor.

13. _____ Because the toaster is broken.

14. _____ Dad put the groceries away.

15. _____ While you were at the mall.

16. _____ A Native American worked on beautiful pottery.

17. _____ After the girls played softball last Saturday.

18. _____ Mrs. Gray's helpfulness was greatly appreciated.

19. _____ During the movie, we ate peanuts and popcorn.

20. _____ Although his voice sounded raspy.

Name_____

Date_____

All clauses contain a subject and a verb.

    A.   An **independent clause** functions as a complete thought. Therefore, it can stand alone as a sentence.

    B.   A **dependent clause** cannot stand alone as a sentence because it doesn't express a complete thought. A **subordinate clause** is a type of dependent clause.

Some sentences contain both a dependent **and** an independent clause. The independent part is often referred to as the main clause. If a subordinating conjunction is used to begin the dependent clause, the entire dependent clause is called a **subordinate clause**.

    Example: **If you will stay**, I'll prepare a snack.

               subordinate   main
                  clause   clause

The main clause may be written first. In this arrangement, no comma is necessary.

    Example: I'll prepare a snack **if you will stay**.

                 main   subordinate
                 clause   clause

Directions: In each sentence, finish the subordinate clause. Write an appropriate main clause.

    Example: _After Lynette **wrote a complimentary letter**_

                to that company, she received free products.

1. <u>Whenever a scientist</u> _____

_____

2. <u>After a hurricane</u> _____

_____

3. <u>Although his reaction</u> _____

_____

4. <u>Before a</u> _____

_____

5. <u>While a trapeze artist</u> _____

_____

6. <u>Until the package</u> _____

_____

7. <u>Since you</u> _____

_____

8. <u>If</u> _____

_____

Name_____

Date_____

All clauses contain a subject and a verb.

    A.   An **independent clause** functions as a complete thought. Therefore, it can stand alone as a sentence.

    B.   A **dependent clause** cannot stand alone as a sentence because it doesn't express a complete thought. A **subordinate clause** is a type of dependent clause.

Some sentences contain both a dependent **and** an independent clause. The

independent part is often referred to as the main clause. If a subordinating conjunction

is used to begin the dependent clause, the entire dependent clause is called a

subordinate clause.

    Example: **Because a ballet troupe will perform**, Teresa and
                          subordinate clause

            I have volunteered to serve on a publicity committee.
                          main clause

The main clause may be written first. In this arrangement, no comma is necessary.

    Example: Teresa and I have volunteered to serve on a publicity committee
                          main clause

            because a ballet troupe will perform.
                    subordinate clause

ő ő ő ő ő

Directions: In each sentence, finish the subordinate clause. Write an appropriate main clause.

    Example: <u>Since Margaret **had traveled in Spain,**</u>

she showed slides to her sister's class.

1. While Mr. Harkins _____

   _____

2. Although their father _____

   _____

3. Before the tornado _____

   _____

4. Whenever the farmer _____

   _____

5. If your _____

   _____

6. Because an explorer _____

   _____

7. As the policeman motioned _____

   _____

368

Name_____

Date_____

A **subordinate clause** contains a **subject** and a **verb**. However, it cannot stand alone as a complete thought. A subordinate clause sounds like someone began to speak and left before he was finished.

> **Example:** **Unless you hurry**

To write a sentence containing a subordinate clause, you can write the subordinating part at the beginning, place a comma, and finish the sentence.

> **Example:** **Unless you hurry,** you may not catch the train.

You may also write the subordinating part after the main thought. A comma is no longer necessary.

> **Example:** You may not catch the train **unless you hurry**.

δ δ δ δ δ

Directions: Finish each sentence.

1. While Dr. Baxter examined the patient _____

   _____

2. If that corporation closes _____

   _____

3.   Although Candace hesitated and sighed _____

_____

4.   As the mountain climber reached the summit _____

_____

5.   If one receives an anonymous phone call _____

_____

6.   When a local mechanic repaired George's automobile _____

_____

7.   After William earned a degree _____

_____

8.   Even though the committee met several times _____

_____

9.   While Janelle distributed papers _____

_____

10. Before Americans won their independence _____

_____

Name_____

Date_____

A **subordinate clause** contains a **subject** and a **verb**. However, it cannot stand alone as a complete thought. A subordinate clause sounds like someone began to speak and left before he was finished.

     Example: **After Randy ate dinner**

To write a sentence containing a subordinate clause, you can write the subordinating part at the beginning, place a comma, and finish the sentence.

     Example: **After Randy ate dinner,** he went to a movie.

You may also write the subordinating part after the main thought. A comma is no longer necessary. For clarity, some words may be moved.

     Example: **Randy went to a movie** after he ate dinner.

Directions: Finish each sentence.

1.   After the goat fled from the barn_____

     _____

2.   When the team ran onto the field_____

     _____

3. If the lemons are fresh _____

    _____

4. Before the man boarded the train _____

    _____

5. Whenever the baby cries _____

    _____

6. Because rain fell in torrents _____

    _____

7. When they arrived _____

    _____

8. Until you learned to walk _____

    _____

9. While some children played hide-and-seek _____

    _____

10. Wherever the horse gallops _____

    _____

Name_____   **SUBORDINATE CLAUSES**

Date_____

As you read, you will note that authors have used subordinate clauses in their writing. Find examples. Write each example and its source.

Sentence: _____

_____

Source: _____

Sentence: _____

_____

Source: _____

Sentence: _____

_____

Source: _____

Sentence: _____

_____

Source: _____

Sentence: _____

_____

Source: _____

🐚 🐚

Sentence: _____

_____

Source: _____

🐚 🐚

Sentence: _____

_____

Source: _____

🐚 🐚

Sentence: _____

_____

Source: _____

🐚 🐚

Sentence: _____

_____

Source: _____

VIII

RELATIVE CLAUSES

Level 2

EFFECTIVE TEACHING: *Refer to page 194.*

IMPORTANT NOTE:

1. Clauses can be confusing. I discuss in this unit the fact that a relative clause may serve as an adjective when it modifies a noun or pronoun in the sentence. A relative clause may also serve as a noun clause when the entire clause serves as a noun.

    > **Example:** The snowboard **that he bought last year** is cracked.
    > *adjective clause*
    > *(modifies snowboard)*

    > **That he is embarrassed** is obvious.
    > *noun clause*
    > *(subject of the sentence)*

2. Sometimes *that* is omitted from the clause. This is allowed if the meaning of the sentence is not altered.

    > **Example:** This is the car **that I want.**
    > This is the car **I want.**

3. Restrictive and nonrestrictive clauses are not discussed. A restrictive clause is essential to the meaning of a sentence and is not set off by commas.

    > **Example:** The judge **who heard the case** sentenced the woman.
    > *restrictive clause*

    A nonrestrictive clause is not essential to the sentence meaning. Commas are needed to set off nonrestrictive clauses.

    > **Example:** His grandfather, **who lives in Idaho,** is a physicist.
    > *nonrestrictive clause*

    <u>**You may wish to teach the entire unit without discussing restrictive and nonrestrictive clauses. After students have mastery of relative clauses, you may want to go back and teach the concept. Students need to determine whether commas should be used.**</u>

A clause is a group of words containing a subject and a verb. A dependent clause

contains subject and verb; however, it cannot stand alone as a complete thought. One

type of dependent clause is a **relative clause**.

>   **Example:**   whom we met

This relative clause begins with the word, **whom**. The subject is *we*; the verb is *met*.

As you can tell, this clause cannot stand alone as a complete thought. More is needed

to make sense.

>   **Example:**   The <u>man</u> **whom we met** <u>is</u> a jockey.

The independent or main clause of the sentence is: *The man is a jockey.*

Whom we met is a special type of dependent clause called a **relative clause**. A

relative clause begins with one of the following words:

>   **who**   **that**
>   **whom**   **which**
>   **whose**

Directions: The subject of the independent (main) clause and a relative clause have
              been written. Complete each sentence.

>   **Example:**   <u>The lady who ordered brocade fabric **will use**</u>
>
>   <u>**it for an evening gown.**</u>

377

1. A telegram that Mom has saved _____

   _____

2. An Indian tribe which lives in the Southwest _____

   _____

3. Their youth director who is from the East _____

   _____

4. Some flowers that had been planted in the spring _____

   _____

5. A house which is over a hundred years old _____

   _____

6. An ocean liner which will sail tomorrow _____

   _____

7. My neighbor who goes to the beach each summer _____

   _____

8. The man whom I had met earlier _____

   _____

A clause is a group of words containing a subject and a verb. A dependent clause contains subject and verb; however, it cannot stand alone as a complete thought. One type of dependent clause is a **relative clause**.

>   **Example:**   that Bill wanted

This relative clause begins with the word, *that*. The subject is *Bill*; the verb is *wanted*. As you can readily discern, this clause cannot stand alone as a complete thought. More is needed to make sense.

>   **Example:**   The <u>shoes</u> **that Bill wanted** <u>were</u> not in stock.

The independent (main) clause of the sentence is: *The shoes were not in stock.*

That Bill wanted is a special type of dependent clause called a **relative clause**.

A relative clause begins with one of the following words:

>   **who**   **that**
>   **whom**   **which**
>   **whose**

Directions: The subject of the independent (main) clause and a relative clause have
              been written. Complete each sentence.

>   **Example:**   <u>The conference which was scheduled for the</u>
>
>   <u>fall **will be postponed.**</u>

1. Beige stationery that she had imprinted _____

   _____

2. The aunt whom we love _____

   _____

3. Martin's son who sings with a barbershop quartet _____

   _____

4. The model whose picture appeared in a fashion magazine _____

   _____

5. The cardboard box which he put under the bed _____

   _____

6. The teacher whose class won a reading contest _____

   _____

7. A state senator who spoke to the women's club _____

   _____

8. The postal lady whom Mrs. Perkins likes _____

   _____

Relative clauses may begin with **who**, **whom**, **whose**, **which**, or **that**. <u>Whoever</u> and <u>whomever</u> are also possibilities.

Relative clauses can serve as nouns in a sentence.

> **Example:**   ***Whoever took my pencil*** needs to return it immediately.
> clause serving as subject of the entire sentence

Relative clauses often serve as adjectives.

> **Example:**   The one ***who finishes first*** is the winner.
> clause serving as adjective describing one

Although this information is interesting, our purpose here is to use relative clauses to add variety and interest to our writing. It is more important to use them as a writing tool than to differentiate their function in the sentence (in these particular lessons.)

δ δ δ δ δ

Directions: Combine the sentences using relative clauses.

> **Example:**   I like music.
>
> The music I like has a message.
>
> **I like music that has a message.**

1.   The teacher called names.
       The names began with <u>R</u>.   (Use **that**)

_____

2. An accident occurred on the freeway.
    The accident was not a serious one.   (Use **which**.)

    _____

    _____

3. Tony gave the paper to Susan.
    Susan suddenly handed it back to him.   (Use **who**.)

    _____

    _____

4. The run-down mill is located on Larkin Road.
    The run-down mill is for sale.   (Use **which**.)

    _____

    _____

5. Brian is a senior.
    Brian was given a scholarship.   (Use **to whom**.)

    _____

    _____

Relative clauses may begin with **who**, **whom**, **whose**, **which**, or **that**. Whoever and whomever are also possibilities.

Relative clauses can serve as nouns in a sentence.

> **Example:**   The dress ***which she chose*** was bright orange with blue dots.
> clause serving as an adjective

Relative clauses often serve as adjectives.

> **Example:**   The winner is ***whoever answers the most questions.***
> clause serving as a predicate nominative

Although this information is interesting, our purpose here is to use relative clauses to add variety and interest to our writing. It is more important to use them as a writing tool than to differentiate their function in the sentence (in these particular lessons.)

🜪 🜪 🜪 🜪 🜪

Directions: Combine the sentences using relative clauses.

> **Example:**   The suit was taken to the cleaners.
> The suit had a spaghetti stain on the sleeve.
>
> The suit which was taken to the cleaners had a spaghetti
> stain on the sleeve.
>
> or
>
> The suit which had a spaghetti stain on the sleeve was taken
> to the cleaners.

1. His niece graduated from Bucknell University.
   She earned her graduate degree from Northern Arizona Univerity.   (Use **who**.)

   _____

   _____

2. A white latticed arch was delivered to the church for a wedding.
   It was covered with white lilies and pink roses.   (Use **that**.)

   _____

   _____

3. The little boy gave his mother a hand-painted noodle necklace.
   He had made the necklace in preschool.   (Use **which**.)

   _____

   _____

4. A tall, dignfied judge entered the courtroom.
   I had met her during another case.   (Use **whom**.)

   _____

   _____

5. The man had been a famous race car driver.
   His son won the Indianapolis 500.   (Use **whose**.)

   _____

   _____

Name_____   **RELATIVE CLAUSES**

Date_____

A **relative clause** contains a subject and a verb. However, it is a dependent clause and, therefore, cannot stand alone as a complete thought.

These words are often used to begin relative clauses:

who

whom

whose

which

that

Directions: Only the subject and the relative word have been written. Finish the relative clause; then, write an appropriate ending that makes sense.

Example: <u>A sign that **appeared in the restaurant's window**</u>

<u>**listed the specials of the day.**</u>

1.   <u>The first grader who</u>_____

_____

2.   <u>This silver dollar that</u>_____

_____

3.   <u>The puzzle which</u>_____

_____

4. A child whose _____

_____

5. The decision that _____

_____

6. An idea which _____

_____

7. She gave the medicine to the nurse whose _____

_____

8. Samantha bought a notebook that _____

_____

9. James's suggestion which _____

_____

10. We talked to a detective who _____

_____

11. A business partner whose _____

_____

Date_____

A **relative clause** contains a subject and a verb. However, it is a dependent clause and, therefore, cannot stand alone as a complete thought.

These words are often used to begin relative clauses: **who**

whom

whose

which

that

Directions: Only the subject and the relative word have been written. Finish the relative clause; then, write an appropriate ending that makes sense.

Example: The mother **whose child starred in the play**

cheered most enthusiastically.

1.   Mr. Kemper's nephew who _____

_____

2.   The emerald ring that _____

_____

3.   The checking account which _____

_____

4. The speaker who _____

    _____

5. Her homework that _____

    _____

6. The point which _____

    _____

7. The baby whose _____

    _____

8. The rug that _____

    _____

9. A pianist who _____

    _____

10. His wishes which _____

    _____

11. The customer who _____

    _____

388

Name_____   **RELATIVE CLAUSES**

Date_____

As you read, you will note that authors have used relative clauses in their writing. Find examples. Write each example and its source.

Sentence: _____

_____

Source: _____

Sentence: _____

_____

Source: _____

Sentence: _____

_____

Source: _____

Sentence: _____

_____

Source: _____

Sentence: _____

_____

Source: _____

Sentence: _____

_____

Source: _____

Sentence: _____

_____

Source: _____

Sentence: _____

_____

Source: _____

Sentence: _____

_____

Source: _____

EDITING SYMBOLS:

> **F**   fragment (not a complete sentence)
>
> **R-O**   run-on sentence
>
> **sp**   spelling   (Circling a word is another editing symbol for a spelling error.)
>
> **P**   punctuation error
>
> **C**   capitalization error
>
> *𝓗*   paragraph   (indent or begin new paragraph)
>
> **K**   awkward   (grammatically correct sentence but sounds wrong or confusing)
>
> **∧**   insert word(s)
>
> **t**   tense error
>
>   delete

Symbols such as *F* and *R-O* are universal; however, one can find variations of most editing marks. In my own classroom, I use the following:

> **w-o**   write-out   (No abbreviations are permitted in formal writing.)
>
> **ts**   topic sentence   (The topic sentence is missing or is not stated clearly.)
>
> **ths**   thesis statement   (The thesis statement is missing or is not stated clearly.)
>
> **sal**   skip a line
>
> **min**   more information needed

hl higher level

*Alone, it means that a higher level sentence structure is needed.

*With a happy face next to it, *hl* reflects that the student has, in fact, used a higher level structure.

voc higher level vocabulary needed

Notes: Because I feel that students need to comprehend editing symbols readily, I require that they learn both the universal symbols and my personal ones immediately. This takes a little quizzing time, but, in the long run, it saves students asking me or each other what a symbol means.

Where to place editing symbols is a matter of personal preference and grade level. Following some publishers' recommendations, one may wish to write in the error for the student. Some teachers prefer to write the editing symbol, especially for punctuation and capitalization, exactly where the mistake has been made. For example, students are provided with the information that an error in punctuation has been made; however, it is their responsibility to discern the type made (colon, comma, etc.). For more advanced students, the symbol is often placed at the beginning of the line where the error occurs.

IRREGULAR VERBS

Infinitive	Present	Past	Present Participle	Past Participle
to be	is, am, are	was, were	being	(had) been
to beat	beat(s)	beat	beating	(had) beaten
to begin	begin(s)	began	beginning	(had) begun
to blow	blow(s)	blew	blowing	(had) blown
to break	break(s)	broke	breaking	(had) broken
to bring	bring(s)	brought	bringing	(had) brought
to burst	burst(s)	burst	bursting	(had) burst
to buy	buy(s)	bought	buying	(had) bought
to choose	choose(s)	chose	choosing	(had) chosen
to come	come(s)	came	coming	(had) come
to do	do, does	did	doing	(had) done
to drink	drink(s)	drank	drinking	(had) drunk
to drive	drive(s)	drove	driving	(had) driven
to eat	eat(s)	ate	eating	(had) eaten
to fall	fall(s)	fell	falling	(had) fallen
to freeze	freeze(s)	froze	freezing	(had) frozen
to give	give(s)	gave	giving	(had) given
to go	go, goes	went	going	(had) gone
to grow	grow(s)	grew	growing	(had) grown

IRREGULAR VERBS

Infinitive	Present	Past	Present Participle	Past Participle
to hang	hang(s)	hanged hung	hanging	(had) hanged (had) hung
to have	have, has	had	having	(had) had
to know	know(s)	knew	knowing	(had) known
to lay	lay(s)	laid	laying	(had) laid
to leave	leave(s)	left	leaving	(had) left
to lie	lie(s)	lay	lying	(had) lain
to ride	ride(s)	rode	riding	(had) ridden
to ring	ring(s)	rang	ringing	(had) rung
to rise	rise(s)	rose	rising	(had) risen
to run	run(s)	ran	running	(had) run
to see	see(s)	saw	seeing	(had) seen
to set	set(s)	set	setting	(had) set
to shake	shake(s)	shook	shaking	(had) shaken
to shrink	shrink(s)	shrank	shrinking	(had) shrunk
to sing	sing(s)	sang	singing	(had) sung
to sink	sink(s)	sank	sinking	(had) sunk
to sit	sit(s)	sat	sitting	(had) sat
to speak	speak(s)	spoke	speaking	(had) spoken
to steal	steal(s)	stole	stealing	(had) stolen
to swear	swear(s)	swore	swearing	(had) sworn

IRREGULAR VERBS

Infinitive	Present	Past	Present Participle	Past Participle
to swim	swim(s)	swam	swimming	(had) swum
to take	take(s)	took	taking	(had) taken
to teach	teach(es)	taught	teaching	(had) taught
to throw	throw(s)	threw	throwing	(had) thrown
to wear	wear(s)	wore	wearing	(had) worn
to write	write(s)	wrote	writing	(had) written

LEVEL 1
ANSWERS

LEVEL 1 ANSWERS: ITEMS IN A SERIES

PAGES 17-18:

ANSWERS MAY VARY SLIGHTLY:

1. Bill and Susan walked to school.
2. Some baby rabbits and deer are in the field.
3. Paper and a blue pen fell to the floor.
4. Her dad and mom played baseball.
5. This plant and tree grew fast.
6. The girls and boys began to sing.
7. Dick and Sally jumped on a hay wagon.
8. Tom and I will go to the library.

PAGES 19-20:

ANSWERS MAY VARY SLIGHTLY:

1. Cars and trucks zoomed down the street.
2. Jody and Dave read a short story.
3. Ann and I dropped popcorn on the floor.
4. A small cup and a big plate had been broken.
5. Blue paint and glue had spilled on the rug.
6. Mark and Tammy played basketball.

PAGES 21-22:

ANSWERS MAY VARY SLIGHTLY:

1. A red airplane and a large jet took off.
2. Mary, Dick, and I stepped on gum.
3. His uncle and aunt have vans.
4. Mrs. Jones, her husband, and their sons baked pies.
5. Barbara and her mother visited London Bridge.
6. Their bikes, skates, and scooters blocked the door.
7. A horse and a cow have long tails.

LEVEL 1 ANSWERS: ITEMS IN A SERIES

PAGES 23-24:

ANSWERS MAY VARY SLIGHTLY:

1. Ed and Donna are always happy.
2. Jack, Josh, and Mike called to me.
3. Sam or Jill ate all the cookies.
4. A mother hen and her little chicks crossed the road.
5. Their brother and sister are good cooks.
6. Her dad or mom may drive us to the game.
7. Her feet and ankles hurt from the long walk.

PAGE 26:

1. like
2. chirp
3. bark
4. ring
5. melt
6. sleep

PAGE 27:

ANSWERS MAY VARY SLIGHTLY:

1. That lady and her father give food to the needy.
2. Bob and his grandpa take piano lessons.
3. The toy boat and the rubber duck float in water.
4. Carl and Tina like to fish at Hornet Lake.

PAGES 29-30:

ANSWERS MAY VARY SLIGHTLY:

1. Fred, Lisa, and Kim like to skate.
2. A dog, a cat, and a little girl play in the yard.
3. A park, a zoo, and a house will be built here.
4. Candy, ice cream, and cake are sweet.
5. Joy, Molly, and I go to dance lessons.

LEVEL 1 ANSWERS: ITEMS IN A SERIES

6.   A bell, an alarm, and a telephone rang.
7.   Miss Jay, Mrs. Loe, and Mr. Dunn wear glasses.

PAGES 31-32:

ANSWERS MAY VARY SLIGHTLY:

1.   Peter hit the ball hard and far.
2.   Uncle Don poured milk and sugar into his coffee.
3.   The sun is large, bright, and hot.
4.   Jack read a book, a magazine, and a newspaper.
5.   Lynn turned on the radio and the television.
6.   Nancy ran into the house, down three steps, and out the back door.
7.   The teacher looked sad and worried.
8.   Erin bought a doll, a baton, and a mirror.

PAGES 33-34:

ANSWERS MAY VARY SLIGHTLY:

1.   A.   Todd and Beth walked to school.
       B.   Both Todd and Beth walked to school.

2.   A.   Those roses and tulips are pretty.
       B.   Both those roses and tulips are pretty.

3.   A.   Her rings and earrings are on that chest.
       B.   Both her rings and earrings are on that chest.

4.   A.   A large ship and a small boat sailed into the bay.
       B.   Both a large ship and a small boat sailed into the bay.

5.   A.   A notebook and pencils are under your bed.
       B.   Both a notebook and pencils are under your bed.

PAGES 35-36:

1.	A and B:	apples	pears
2.	A and B:	girls	boys
3.	A and B:	house	barn
4.	A and B:	Billy	mother
5.	A and B:	robins	sparrows

LEVEL 1 ANSWERS: ITEMS IN A SERIES

PAGES 37-38:

ANSWERS MAY VARY SLIGHTLY:

1. A. An owl and a swallow sat in a tall oak tree
   B. Both an owl and a swallow sat in a tall oak tree.

2. A. Rob and his friend ate breakfast.
   B. Both Rob and his friend ate breakfast.

3. A. A squirrel and a chipmunk played on the lawn.
   B. Both a squirrel and a chipmunk played on the lawn.

4. A. Joey and Mindy ran to the swings.
   B. Both Joey and Mindy ran to the swings.

PAGES 39-40:

ANSWERS MAY VARY SLIGHTLY:

1. A. Both pizza and tacos will be served.
   B. Not only pizza but also tacos will be served.

2. A. Both her family and friends came to the party.
   B. Not only her family but also her friends came to the party.

3. A. Both a mailman and a saleman came to our door.
   B. Not only a mailman but also a saleman came to our door.

4. A. Both a fly and a bee flew around them.
   B. Not only a fly but also a bee flew around them.

5. A. Both Nick and his older sister won a contest.
   B. Not only Nick but also his older sister won a contest.

402

LEVEL 1 ANSWERS: ITEMS IN A SERIES

PAGES 41-42:

ANSWERS MAY VARY SLIGHTLY:

1. A. Both pins and needles were on the floor.
   B. Not only pins but also needles were on the floor.

2. A. Both Dave and Paul ate steak.
   B. Not only Dave but also Paul ate steak.

3. A. Both Mrs. Thomas and Mr. Thomas knitted sweaters.
   B. Not only Mrs. Thomas but also Mr. Thomas knitted sweaters.

4. A. Both this buzzer and that alarm rang loudly.
   B. Not only this buzzer but also that alarm rang loudly.

5. A. Both her friend and her sister left early.
   B. Not only her friend but also her sister left early.

6. A. Both Jan and Bob looked strangely at me.
   B. Not only Jan but also Bob looked strangely at me.

PAGE 43:

ANSWERS MAY VARY SLIGHTLY:

1. Pam drives a car or a van.
2. Joe decided to swing or to slide.
3. The family is going to a lake or to the river.
4. Those cups are dirty or tea-stained.

LEVEL 1 ANSWERS: ITEMS IN A SERIES

PAGES 45-46:

ANSWERS MAY VARY SLIGHTLY:

1. Either your penny or your dime is under the table.
2. Either a cup or a dish has been broken.
3. Either a toy or a game had been given as a prize.
4. Either a kite or a paper airplane could be made in art class.
5. Either Miss Hobbs or Mr. Flint teaches Sunday school.
6. Either my aunt or my uncle will take us to the zoo.
7. Either flower seeds or pumpkin seeds are planted there.
8. Either Sparky or some birds ate the dog food.

PAGES 47-48:

ANSWERS MAY VARY SLIGHTLY:

1. Either milk or tea will be served.
2. Either Bob or Joy lives there.
3. Either crayons or colored pencils may be used.
4. Either my mom or dad will make lunch.
5. Either shoes or sandals must be worn.
6. Either a dog or cat ran into our house.
7. Either Mark or his sister is first on the slide.

Note: Students need to understand that with *either-or* construction, the verb must agree with the closer subject in sentences using the present tense.

LEVEL 1 ANSWERS: SEMICOLON CONSTRUCTION

PAGES 53-54:

1.	S	10.	S	1.	sad face
2.	NS	11.	NS	2.	happy face
3.	NS	12.	NS	3.	sad face
4.	S	13.	NS	4.	happy face
5.	NS	14.	NS		
6.	NS	15.	S		
7.	S				
8.	NS				
9.	NS				

PAGES 55-56:

ANSWERS MAY VARY SLIGHTLY:

1.   Her kitten is playing; he is chasing a ball.
2.   We rode on a new bus; it is red and blue.
3.   Kent will not go; therefore, I will not go either.
4.   The bag tore; therefore, a can of soup fell on the floor.
5.   Sam and Nan love math; they like to add the most.
6.   I love turkey; however, I dislike the dark meat.
7.   That pencil will not work; however, you may use mine.

PAGES 57-58:

ANSWERS MAY VARY SLIGHTLY:

1.   Their keys are lost; therefore, they are locked out.
2.   We want to go; however, our parents won't let us.
3.   Cotton candy is good; however, it is bad for our teeth.
4.   We won the game; therefore, we went for pizza.
5.   Her hair was sticky; therefore, she washed it.
6.   Mark is small for his age; however, he is very good at sports.
7.   A glass broke; therefore, do not walk in the kitchen until it is cleaned.
8.   They like to camp; therefore, their family went to the lake.
9.   That is my best teddy bear; however, the dog chewed its ear.

LEVEL 1 ANSWERS: SEMICOLON CONSTRUCTION

PAGES 59-60:

ANSWERS WILL VARY:
REPRESENTATIVE ANSWERS:

1.   This milk is sour; therefore, it must be thrown away.
2.   A parade came down the street; the crowd cheered as it passed.
3.   It rained all day; therefore, George and I enjoyed inside games.
4.   The teacher is happy; all of his students are working hard.
5.   Jan picked up a ball; however, she dropped it when she realized it was wet.
6.   His dad like to cook; therefore, he makes dinner twice a week.
7.   This floor is dirty; however, no one has time to wash it.
8.   Today is very cold; it is snowing.
9.   A bus stopped at the corner, however, no one got off.

PAGES 61-62:

ANSWERS WILL VARY:
REPRESENTATIVE ANSWERS:

1.   Dogs are fun; however, you must take care of them.
2.   My friend is nice; therefore, I like being with her.
3.   This bike is broken; Trina will fix it this afternoon.
4.   Sally drew a picture; however, she would not put it up.
5.   These fries are cold; therefore, they must be heated.
6.   Ken opened the door; a cold gust of wind blew in.
7.   This teddy bear is soft; therefore, I like to sleep with it.
8.   Mom's birthday is this week; we will bake her a cake.

PAGES 63-64:

ANSWERS WILL VARY:
REPRESENTATIVE ANSWERS:

1.   A parade marched by; we had fun watching it.
2.   Your shoe is on the floor; place it in your closet, please.

LEVEL 1 ANSWERS: SEMICOLON CONSTRUCTION

3. Jane asked a question; however, her mother did not answer it.
4. Trash is all over the street; someone needs to pick it up.
5. The train stopped suddenly; its brakes screeched.
6. Today is very hot; let's go swimming.
7. James is sitting in the corner; he is pouting because he wants candy.
8. The player ran to the end of the field; however, he did not catch the ball.
9. This apple pie smells good; therefore, we will eat it while it is still warm.
10. Larry's aunt will visit next week; she will fly in from Texas.
11. Todd wrote a letter; however, he forgot the stamp.
12. This book has many pictures; therefore, it is fun to read.

LEVEL 1 ANSWERS: APPOSITIVES

ANSWERS MAY VARY SLIGHTLY:

1.   Dr. Hand, **my dentist**, looks at my teeth.
2.   Harry went to Globe, **a town in Arizona**.
3.   The farmer stood next to Millie, **a cow**.
4.   Katy, **a good softball player**, hit a home run.
5.   Troy, **my cousin**, is on the track team.
6.   Linn bought a drink, **a banana milkshake.**
7.   His mother, **an artist**, draws horses.
8.   This book, **a science fiction novel**, is Ted's.
9.   Pat shared his lunch, **a peanut butter and jelly sandwich.**

ANSWERS MAY VARY SLIGHTLY:

1.   Todd's uncle gave me a gift, **a yellow kite**.
2.   This book, **a mystery**, is good.
3.   His favorite food, **pizza**, will be served for lunch.
     (Technically, commas are not required for one word appositives.)
4.   Cindy, **my friend**, lives next door.
5.   Sparky, **a puppy**, licks my hand.
6.   Lalita, **my aunt**, is visiting us.
7.   The desserts, **pie and cake**, are on the table.
8.   Mom won a prize, **a red and white dish**.
9.   Mrs. Barnes, **a Sunday school teacher**, gave me a sticker.

ANSWERS MAY VARY SLIGHTLY:

1.   Fido, **my dog**, likes to chew bones.
2.   Bob, **my brother**, races cars.
3.   Joan, **Sandy's friend**, lives in New York.
4.   He rode Mr. Carter's horse, **a brown mare**.
5.   The building, **an orange barn**, was torn down.
6.   Mr. Reed, **our minister**, comes to visit us.
7.   Fluffy, **a French poodle**, jumps around too much.
8.   Timmy ate fruit, **two apples and a pear**, for lunch.
9.   Two stuffed animals, **a bear and a pig**, are on the bed.

LEVEL 1 ANSWERS: PARTICIPIAL PHRASES
PRESENT PARTICIPLE CONSTRUCTION

PAGE 79:

1.	finding	11.	passing
2.	dancing	12.	meeting
3.	pulling	13.	asking
4.	baking	14.	stirring
5.	spending	15.	letting
6.	tapping	16.	knowing
7.	speaking	17.	throwing
8.	living	18.	finishing
9.	making	19.	crying
10.	seeing	20.	shouting

PAGES 81-82:

ANSWERS WILL VARY:
REPRESENTATIVE ANSWERS:

1.	hopping in a game	21.	sleeping late
2.	running down the street	22.	smiling and waving
3.	playing with his sister	23.	drinking a cup of water
4.	reading a book		
5.	flying in an airplane		
6.	eating pickles		
7.	picking apples		
8.	hiding behind a bush		
9.	washing clothes		
10.	taking her lunch		
11.	sending a card		
12.	opening a can		
13.	hitting a ball		
14.	being a nice person		
15.	writing a letter		
16.	laughing at the joke		
17.	planting a garden		
18.	riding a horse		
19.	falling down		
20.	looking for a job		

LEVEL 1 ANSWERS: PARTICIPIAL PHRASES
PRESENT PARTICIPLE CONSTRUCTION

PAGES 83-84:

ANSWERS WILL VARY:
REPRESENTATIVE ANSWERS:

1. Eating pizza, the small child burned his lip.
2. Counting the money, the teller talked about her vacation.
3. Fishing in a stream, Sandy and Todd caught three trout.
4. Stopping the car, Bobby checked the tires.
5. Making pancakes, Jill flipped one in the air.
6. Smelling pepper, Helen sneezed.
7. Lying on the floor, the girl is reading a magazine.

PAGES 85-86:

ANSWERS WILL VARY:
REPRESENTATIVE ANSWERS:

1. Looking for his jacket, Brian lifted the couch cushions.
2. Pretending to be a duck, Patty waddled across the room.
3. Trying to climb a hill, the hiker panted and stopped.
4. Sharing her lunch, Barbara handed her friends some cookies.
5. Hanging a poster in his room, Scott stood back to look at it.
6. Chewing gum, the bus driver chomped harder as he went faster.
7. Petting his kitten, the boy lay on his bed and watched television.
8. Sitting on the bank of a stream, the fisherman cast his line out into the middle.
9. Hoping for a red wagon for her birthday, Julie looked at a picture of one.

PAGES 87-88:

ANSWERS WILL VARY:
REPRESENTATIVE ANSWERS:

1. Sitting in a chair, Miss Blake read the newspaper.
2. Reaching for a cookie, the little boy stood on his tiptoes.
3. Skating on a frozen pond, Missy and her friend played hockey.
4. Setting the table, Timmy put all the knives on the plates.
5. Playing a game of softball, we were first batters.

LEVEL 1 ANSWERS: PARTICIPIAL PHRASES
PRESENT PARTICIPLE CONSTRUCTION

6. Hearing its name called, the puppy ran to its owner.
7. Hanging a picture on the wall, their parents did not agree if it were crooked.
8. Making a sandwich, Mike buttered two slices of bread.

PAGES 89-90:

ANSWERS WILL VARY:
REPRESENTATIVE ANSWERS:

1. Talking on the telephone, Gail munched on chips.
2. Diving off the board, the boy did a bellyflop.
3. Beating on a drum, the girl marched with a band.
4. Racing her bike, Glenda pedaled very fast.
5. Waving to their friends, they boarded the airplane.
6. Tripping over a tin can, Pat lunged forward.
7. Walking in a parade, the girls were dressed as chickens.
8. Making my own breakfast, I buttered toast and made oatmeal.
9. Dropping her pencil, Lisa stopped to pick it up.

PAGES 91-92:

ANSWERS WILL VARY:
REPRESENTATIVE ANSWERS:

1. Smiling at the baby, Jack pulled its toes.
2. Slipping on ice, I skidded three feet.
3. Writing on the wall, the art class finished their project.
4. Pulling a wagon, an elderly man walked toward the food bank.
5. Turning on the light, we could see our way up the stairs.
6. Stopping the ball, Herman threw it to first for the out.
7. Playing tag, the children dashed through the yard.
8. Acting like a monster, Jimmy is scaring everyone.
9. Leaning back in his chair, the businessman throught carefully about the decision.

LEVEL 1 ANSWERS: PARTICIPIAL PHRASES
PRESENT PARTICIPLE CONSTRUCTION

PAGES 93-94:

ANSWERS WILL VARY:
REPRESENTATIVE ANSWERS:
*

1. Jim, making a dash for the door, bumped into his mother.
2. The club, choosing a new president, voted by secret ballot.
3. Jane's dad, wearing a heavy coat, was ready for the sleigh ride.
4. A policeman, helping a lost child, asked the clerk to page the child's parents.
5. Mandy, smelling smoke, checked the house carefully for fire.
6. Five boys, rushing through the door at the same time, fell over each other.
7. The baby, crying loudly, wanted to be fed.
8. A large spider, spinning a fine web, came out after dark.
9. A student, thinking aloud, distracted his neighbor who was taking a test.
10. Her pet sheep, following her around the farm, was a comic sight.
11. A loud noise, sounding like an airplane flying low, woke their entire family.

PAGES 95-96:

ANSWERS WILL VARY:
REPRESENTATIVE ANSWERs:
*

1. The dog, lying in the grass, is chewing a bone.
2. A cat, eating food, looked up.
3. The boy, playing baseball, hit a home run.
4. Kirk's dad, washing his car, is talking to his friend.
5. Miss Sands, looking for her lost hamster, appears upset.

PAGES 97-98:

ANSWERS WILL VARY:
REPRESENTATIVE ANSWERS:
*

1. The man, sitting in his truck, is writing a letter.
2. Their sister, baking cookies, burned herself on the hot pan.
3. The family, going on vacation, has the dog in the car.
4. The child, crying for his mother, stood in the middle of the floor.
5. Lana, laughing at her brother, bumped into the wall.
*See the note on page 452 regarding commas.
412

PAGES 103-104:

1. played
2. fixed
3. watched
4. pasted
5. skipped
6. loved
7. clapped
8. lifted
9. baked
10. hugged
11. parked
12. cleaned
13. washed
14. painted

to bark	(had) barked
to hand	(had) handed
to rub	(had) rubbed
to stop	(had) stopped
to laugh	(had) laughed

PAGES 105-106:

1. painted
2. chewed
3. jumped
4. cooked

LEVEL 1 ANSWERS: PARTICIPIAL PHRASES
PAST PARTCIPLE CONSTRUCTION

5.   opened
6.   fished
7.   walked
8.   liked
9.   pretended
10. handed
11. mopped
12. patted
13. rested
14. pressed
15. rinsed

to spell	(had) spelled
to wrap	(had) wrapped
to dip	(had) dipped
to kick	(had) kicked
to print	(had) printed
to believe	(had) believed

PAGES 107-108:

1.   ridden
2.   sung
3.   rung
4.   given
5.   sent
6.   driven
7.   spoken

414

8. eaten
9. fallen
10. stolen
11. found
12. seen
13. gone
14. chosen
15. taken

to freeze	(had) frozen
to throw	(had) thrown
to write	(had) written
to know	(had) known
to sit	(had) sat

PAGES 109-110:

1. (had) parked
   a parked car

2. (had) frozen
   a frozen pond

3. (had) burned
   burned cookies

4. (had) stolen
   a stolen automobile

5. (had) written
   a written message

6. (had) rented
   that rented vehicle

7. (had) ripped
   a ripped shirt

8. (had) lost
   a lost animal

9. (had) wrapped
   her wrapped package

10. (had) fried
    fried chicken

11. (had) sprained
    a sprained ankle

PAGES 111-112:

1. (had) spilled
   spilled milk

2. (had) peeled
   peeled potatoes

3. (had) returned
   a returned letter

4. (had) hurt
   a hurt finger

5. (had) faded
   faded jeans

6. (had) spoiled
   a spoiled child

7. (had) tired
   the tired hiker

8. (had) covered
   a covered wagon

9. (had) scared
   a scared person

10. (had) packed
    a packed lunch

11. (had) softened
    softened butter

LEVEL 1 ANSWERS: PARTICIPIAL PHRASES
PAST PARTCIPLE CONSTRUCTION

PAGES 113-114:

1. combed hair
   Combed, his hair looked sharp.

2. a locked gate
   Locked, the gate was a good way to keep out unwanted visitors.

3. a repeated message
   Repeated, the message was more easily understood.

4. melted cheese
   Melted, the cheese oozed all over the plate.

5. a frozen dessert
   Frozen, the icy dessert hurt his teeth.

6. a stolen bike
   Stolen, the blue bike had been found in a woods.

PAGES 115-116:

1. a lost dog
   Lost, the dog wandered through the streets.

2. a spained ankle
   Sprained, her ankle swelled and hurt.

3. a relaxed person
   Relaxed, Debra lay down on the floor to read.

4. an excited child
   Excited, the child jumped up and down.

5.   cooked vegetables
      Cooked, the vegetables were soft and tasty.

6.   a painted face
      Painted, his face looked like a clown.

PAGES 117-118:

1.   a written message
      Written, the message explained why Susie had been absent on Monday.

2.   a raised flag
      Raised, the flag waved in the wind.

3.   a trusted friend
      Trusted, the man was given a large sum of money to hold.

4.   filled stockings
      Filled, the stockings were heavy with gifts.

5.   a broken wagon
      Broken, the wagon lay in pieces.

6.   a hidden camera
      Hidden, the camera takes pictures of people at the bank.

PAGE 120:

ANSWERS WILL VARY:
REPRESENTATIVE ANSWERS:

1.   Taken to the principal, the child received an award for good behavior.
2.   Locked in a car, the keys were lying on the floor.
3.   Driven at a high speed, the car swerved dangerously.

LEVEL 1 ANSWERS: PARTICIPIAL PHRASES
PAST PARTCIPLE CONSTRUCTION

4.   Followed by a mean dog, I ran home.
5.   Made of wool, the shirt is warm.
6.   Thrown over the fence, a bottle landed in our yard.
7.   Placed in a sink, the baby was given a bath.

PAGE 122:

ANSWERS WILL VARY:
REPRESENTATIVE ANSWERS:

1.   Baked for a whole hour, his cookies were black.
2.   Scrubbed clean, the floor was shiny.
3.   Chased by two girls, the boy ran to his friends.
4.   Chosen the winner, Mike's team cheered.
5.   Taught how to swim, the child was not afraid of the water.
6.   Yelled at for being late, Brenda went to her room.
7.   Finished with their work, Mom and Dad rested.

PAGES 123-124:

ANSWERS WILL VARY:
REPRESENTATIVE ANSWERS:

1.   The company, begun in 1960, closed its doors.
2.   The team, defeated again, walked slowly off the field.
3.   Her dime, dropped on the floor, rolled behind a chair.
4.   A rabbit, huddled in a corner, ate some lettuce.
5.   The teacher, surprised by the students, smiled and hugged them.
6.   His hair, brushed well, was smooth.
7.   The cat, curled up on a bed, slept comfortably.
8.   The book, read nightly, was exciting.
9.   The car, broken down in the driveway, rested on cement blocks.
10.   Their vacation, spent in a tent, was peaceful.
11.   Her birthday party, held at a pizza place, was noisy.
12.   The dog, trained to shake hands, put his paw forward.

LEVEL 1 ANSWERS: PARTICIPIAL PHRASES
PAST PARTCIPLE CONSTRUCTION

PAGES 125-126:

ANSWERS WILL VARY:
REPRESENTATIVE ANSWERS:

1. The singers, led by Miss Smith, practiced for their program.
2. A white cake, frosted with pink icing, was cut and served.
3. The dollar bill, torn into two pieces, was taped back together.
4. Candy, eaten before dinner, can ruin your appetite.
5. Her hair, pulled back into a ponytail, bounced as she walked.
6. His sack lunch, laid on a chair, was smashed.
7. A heart, carved out of wood, was painted red.
8. A coat, found on the playground, was turned in to the office.
9. Cookies, decorated with red sprinkles, were made for Valentine's Day.
10. The ball, hit to second base, rolled past the player.
11. The child, reminded to do his chore, frowned.
12. Two pictures, pasted to a paper, showed Jackie's vacation.

LEVEL 1 ANSWERS: HAVING + PAST PARTICIPLE CONSTRUCTION

PAGES 131-132:

1. walked
2. gone
3. yelled
4. eaten
5. pulled
6. sailed
7. smiled
8. done
9. liked
10. stayed
11. left
12. seen
13. hunted
14. torn
15. found

PAGES 133-134:

1. chased
2. smelled
3. given
4. ridden
5. finished
6. looked
7. printed
8. run
9. broken
10. placed
11. filled
12. cut
13. drunk
14. folded

LEVEL 1 ANSWERS: HAVING + PAST PARTICIPLE CONSTRUCTION

PAGE 136:

ANSWERS WILL VARY:
REPRESENTATIVE ANSWERS:

1. Having bent a nail, the girl tried to straighten it.
2. Having blown up a balloon, he was out of breath.
3. Having hit the ball, the batter ran to first base.
4. Having thrown a rattle, the laughing baby kicked her legs.
5. Having rolled a toy car, Eric crawled across the room after it.
6. Having lost his money, the boy looked for it.
7. Having traveled for a day, the children were sleepy.
8. Having shopped happily, they piled their bags into the car's trunk.

PAGE 138:

ANSWERS WILL VARY:
REPRESENTATIVE ANSWERS:

1. Having won the game, the team cheered.
2. Having eaten a meal, Sarah washed the dishes.
3. Having found his favorite teddy bear, the child hugged it.
4. Having seen the movie, the actress cried.
5. Having gathered nuts, the squirrel sat on a tree limb.
6. Having worked all night, her dad went to bed.
7. Having eaten some cereal, Ken went to work.

PAGES 139-140:

ANSWERS WILL VARY:
REPRESENTATIVE ANSWERS:

1. Having made brownies, Larry and Sue washed the bowl.
2. Having stopped suddenly, Panya lost her balance.
3. Having eaten a banana split, Janice went out to play.
4. Having fallen, I skinned my knee.
5. Having swum all day, they decided to stay home.
6. Having cooked dinner, Mother washed the pans.

422

LEVEL 1 ANSWERS: HAVING + PAST PARTICIPLE CONSTRUCTION

7.   Having earned twenty dollars, we bought two books.
8.   Having helped his grandmothr, Steve drove home.

PAGES 141-142:

ANSWERS WILL VARY:
REPRESENTATIVE ANSWERS:

1.   Having yelled, the boy was hoarse.
2.   Having found a quarter, the little girl put it in her pocket.
3.   Having done their homework, Bob and Tom played checkers.
4.   Having washed his bike, Fred wiped it with a towel.
5.   Having sung three songs, we sat down.
6.   Having tripped over a rock, Miss Hanks stubbed her toe.
7.   Having run out of the yard, the puppy chased a car.
8.   Having taken a bath, the two children put on pajamas.
9.   Having seen a snake, I ran.

PAGES 143-144:

ANSWERS WILL VARY:
REPRESENTATIVE ANSWER:

1.   Having washed all the windows, he put away his ladder.
2.   Having had a bad dream, Lulu woke up crying.
3.   Having scared their friend, the boys laughed.
4.   Having colored a picture, the first grader gave it to his mom.
5.   Having bought some candy, Jamilla shared it.
6.   Having given his friend a hat, Aren watched him put it on.
7.   Having moved to a farm, they were given a horse.
8.   Having heard a siren, the driver pulled over to the side of the road.
9.   Having dropped an ice cream cone, I cleaned it off the sidewalk.
10.   Having brushed her teeth, Chika went to bed.
11.   Having sat on wet paint, the lady stood up and moaned.

LEVEL 1 ANSWERS: HAVING + PAST PARTICIPLE CONSTRUCTION

PAGES 145-146:

ANSWERS WILL VARY:
REPRESENTATIVE ANSWERS:

1. Having dropped a dime, I looked for it under the sofa.
2. Having listened carefully, Linda knew exactly what to do.
3. Having set the box on the table, Mrs. Patters opened it.
4. Having fixed the car, Amy drove it to the store.
5. Having fallen out of bed, she bumped her head.
6. Having rollerskated for four hours, their legs were tired.
7. Having helped the older man from the car, a kind nurse led him into his home.
8. Having missed the bus, Henry went home to call his dad.
9. Having built a fort, everyone played in it for hours.
10. Having stubbed her toe, Lily cried out in pain.
11. Having called for help, we waited for the paramedics to arrive.

LEVEL 1 ANSWERS: SUBORDINATE CLAUSES

PAGES 152-153:

1.	man	licked
2.	you	eat
3.	lights	dimmed
4.	I	ate
5.	sister	plays
6.	cat	likes
7.	Mike	washed
8.	dog	drank
9.	Dad	leaves
10.	aunt	drives

1.	
2.	√
3.	√
4.	√
5.	
6.	√
7.	√
8.	
9.	√
10.	√

PAGES 156-157:

1.	ball	rolled
2.	Henry	likes
3.	it	snows
4.	boys	are
5.	we	leave
6.	yard	is
7.	ice	melts
8.	bow	is
9.	Dennis	brushes
10.	horse	likes

LEVEL 1 ANSWERS: SUBORDINATE CLAUSES

1. ___
2. ___
3. √
4. ___
5. √
6. ___
7. √
8. ___
9. √
10. ___

PAGE 158:

1. DC√
2. IC
3. DC√
4. IC
5. DC√
6. IC
7. IC
8. IC
9. DC√

PAGE 159:

1. DC
2. IC
3. DC
4. IC
5. DC
6. DC
7. DC
8. IC

LEVEL 1 ANSWERS: SUBORDINATE CLAUSES

PAGE 160:

1. DC
2. IC
3. DC
4. DC
5. DC
6. DC
7. IC
8. IC

PAGES 161-162:

ANSWERS WILL VARY:
REPRESENTATIVE ANSWERS:

1. When Tina smiles, she shows her beautiful white teeth.
2. Before Tim leaves, he always locks the door.
3. If I were you, I would try again.
4. Because Mrs. Samson likes cheese, she bought three pounds.
5. Unless my homework is finished, I can't watch television.
6. After we went to the store, we put away our groceries.
7. Until the bus comes, they talk every morning.
8. Whenever Grandpa comes to visit, he brings his golf clubs.
9. As Sarah was walking to her friend's house, she stopped to pick some flowers.

PAGES 163-164:

ANSWERS WILL VARY:
REPRESENTATIVE ANSWERS:

1. Although his ankle was hurt, the player finished the game.
2. When Marty grows up, he wants to be a forest ranger.
3. If the rain stops, let's go out and play.
4. After Gregg and Sue chopped wood, they stacked it against the house.
5. Although Helen is sick, she stays up very late.
6. As the play began, Rob started to squirm in his seat.
7. Unless the team wins the next game, it will not be in the championships.

427

LEVEL 1 ANSWERS: SUBORDINATE CLAUSES

8.   Whenever John sneezes, he always covers his nose and mouth.
9.   Because Fred runs fast, he will beat Molly.

PAGES 165-166:

ANSWERS WILL VARY:
REPRESENTATIVE ANSWERS:

1.   When the buzzer sounded, Mom removed clothes from the dryer.
2.   After I ate breakfast, I went to the post office.
3.   When I was a baby, I was so cute.
4.   Because the toy is broken, it must be thrown away.
5.   Before we go to bed, we brush our teeth.
6.   If it rains, our class will play inside.
7.   Although I was tired, my goal of completing the lesson was achieved.
8.   Whenever Billy laughs, he hides his head.
9.   Since you finished first, you may help me.

PAGES 173-175:

1. <u>dad</u>   <u>laughed</u>
2. <u>Tom</u>   <u>goes</u>
3. <u>horse</u>   <u>stood</u>
4. <u>girls</u>   <u>played</u>
5. <u>horn</u>   <u>blew</u>
6. <u>Jason</u>   <u>dropped</u>
7. <u>garden</u>   <u>has</u>
8. <u>friend</u>   <u>listens</u>

ANSWERS MAY VARY:

1. The bird that sits on our roof is a pigeon.
2. The apple which rolled under the table needs to be washed.
3. Her cousin who is in the army will come home for the holidays.
4. A lady whom we saw reminded us of Aunt Bertha.
5. The tree that was cut down was used for firewood.
6. A baby whose picture had been taken was restless.
7. The actor who was the star of the show would not give autographs.

PAGES 177-179:

1. <u>child</u>   <u>washed</u>
2. <u>grandma</u>   <u>likes</u>
3. <u>ring</u>   <u>is</u>
4. <u>They</u>   <u>sang</u>
5. <u>car</u>   <u>stopped</u>

ANSWERS MAY VARY:

1. The lady who called my mother was Miss Bart.
2. The box that is in the corner belongs to Rena.
3. Some plants that need more water should be planted here.
4. Her bedroom which is a mess needs to be cleaned.
5. The boy whom we saw at the store is Tara's brother.
6. Their friend who lives next door to me is twelve.

7.   The boy whose picture won first place wants to be an artist.
8.   The necklace that is silver and stone was made by a Native American.
9.   Linda's aunt who is visiting wants to meet you.
10. Games that are long can be fun.

PAGES 181-182:

ANSWERS WILL VARY:
REPRESENTATIVE ANSWERS:

1.   Christopher found a suitcase that had been stolen.
2.   The lady who just got in line is my mother.
3.   This poem that is best will be read to the class.
4.   We have a new friend who is from Utah.
5.   The baby whose picture was taken is my cousin.
6.   The bag which is on the table contains candy.

PAGES 183-184:

ANSWERS WILL VARY:
REPRESENTATIVE ANSWERS:

1.   Uncle Bob makes good chicken that has been dipped in batter.
2.   At the store, Dale saw a girl who is in his Sunday school class.
3.   The boys and girls built a snowman that has twigs for arms.
4.   The boy whose tennis shoes are black is my brother.
5.   Those flowers which are on the table are from our garden.
6.   His aunt is a designer who creates unusual opal jewelry.

PAGES 185-186:

ANSWERS WILL VARY:
REPRESENTATIVE ANSWERS:

1.   I gave the book to Tim who returned it to the library.
2.   The lake that is near our town is very small.
3.   My friend who takes ballet lessons likes to dance.

4. The park which has just been finished is near their home.
5. The trip that Jack and Emma took was very exciting.
6. The man whose grandfather likes railroads bought a steam engine calendar.
7. I saw a girl who looks very much like my cousin.
8. The pen that Eric lost is blue.
9. I found the keys which had been misplaced for two weeks.

1. whom
2. whom

PAGES 187-188:

ANSWERS WILL VARY:
REPRESENTATIVE ANSWERS:

1. My answer which was incorrect sounded right.
2. Frank's aunt who is forty-five returned to college.
3. The glasses that were broken had been left on the floor.
4. The shopper whose ticket was drawn won a bag of groceries.
5. The person who sells the most will receive a prize.
6. A light that blinks may have a short in it.
7. The player to whom the award was given was a good sport.
8. Troy has a grandfather who rode broncos in rodeos.
9. His toy which lights up is a revolving top.
10. An actor whose last movie was a hit flew to New York for a talk show.
11. The plumber for whom Jack works lives in a nearby town.

LEVEL 2
ANSWERS

LEVEL 2 ANSWERS: ITEMS IN A SERIES

PAGES 195-196:

ANSWERS MAY VARY SLIGHTLY:

1. Bricks, concrete, and tiles were used on the patio.
2. Front desk representatives, valet parking attendants, and reservationists attended the hotel meeting.
3. Tin cans, broken bottles, and torn newspapers were scattered in the vacant lot.
4. Mike, Bobbi Jo, and Tracey scored well on the math exam.
5. The bank teller, the loan officer, and the receptionist seemed uneasy.
6. Their television, radio, and stereo have been repaired.
7. Jane's father, her brother, and her uncle are ministers.
8. The Carter family, the Gibson family, and we are going to the beach.
9. Linguini, fettucini, and lasagna were featured for lunch.
10. Small baskets of pink flowers, crepe paper streamers, and satin bows adorned the bridal table.

PAGE 197:

ANSWERS MAY VARY SLIGHTLY:

1. Reference books, magazines and fiction books can be found in the library.
2. Boxes, luggage, and water skis had been piled in the hallway.
3. Rice, noodles, or mashed potatoes will be served for dinner.
4. Cowboys, cowgirls, and clowns are riding horses in the rodeo parade.
5. John's truck, Jan's van, or Mindy's station wagon may be used for the trip.

PAGES 199-200:

ANSWERS MAY VARY SLIGHTLY:

1. A. The pitcher and the catcher hit a ball to right field.
   B. Both the pitcher and the catcher hit a ball to right field.

2. A. These chopped apples and these bananas are for your cereal.
   B. Both these chopped apples and these bananas are for your cereal.

3. A. A wooden duck and a totem pole had been carved by the same artist.
   B. Both a wooden duck and a totem pole had been carved by the same artist.

435

LEVEL 2 ANSWERS: ITEMS IN A SERIES

4.   A.   That red building and the one beside it will be renovated.
      B.   Both that red building and the one beside it will be renovated.
5.   A.   A manicure and a pedicure were given to the salon's client.
      B.   Both a manicure and a pedicure were given to the salon's client.

PAGES 201-202:

ANSWERS MAY VARY SLIGHTLY:

1.   A.   Crickets and grasshoppers hopped through the tall grass.
      B.   Both crickets and grasshoppers hopped through the tall grass.

2.   A.   A kangaroo and a koala are Australian marsupials.
      B.   Both a kangaroo and a koala are Australian marsupials.

3.   A.   Nanette's younger brother and her cousin play the piano.
      B.   Both Nanette's younger brother and her cousin play the piano.

4.   A.   Corsica and Sardinia are islands east of Italy.
      B.   Both Corsica and Sardinia are islands east of Italy.

5.   A.   A brush and a currycomb are used to groom a horse.
      B.   Both a brush and a currycomb are used to groom a horse.

6.   A.   An egret and a heron waded in shallow water.
      B.   Both an egret and a heron waded in shallow water.

PAGES 203-204:

ANSWERS MAY VARY SLIGHTLY:

1.   A.   Seaweed and a piece of driftwood floated to the shore.
      B.   Both seaweed and a piece of driftwood floated to the shore.

2.   A.   Arizona and New Mexico were admitted to the Union in 1912.
      B.   Both Arizona and New Mexico were admitted to the Union in 1912.

3.   A.   The school play and the program had been written by Steve Platt.
      B.   Both the school play and the program had been written by Steve Platt.

LEVEL 2 ANSWERS: ITEMS IN A SERIES

4.   A.   Her credit card and her keys were lying on the desk.
      B.   Both her credit card and her keys were lying on the desk.

5.   A.   Georgia and Alabama border the state of Florida.
      B.   Both Georgia and Alabama border the state of Florida.

PAGES 205-206:

ANSWERS MAY VARY SLIGHTLY:

1.   A.   Wind and sleet slashed at my face.
      B.   Both wind and sleet slashed at my face.
      C.   Not only wind but also sleet slashed at my face.

2.   A.   Cottage cheese and peaches had been served for lunch.
      B.   Both cottage cheese and peaches had been served for lunch.
      C.   Not only cottage cheese but also peaches had been served for lunch.

3.   A.   Geese and robins are flying south for the winter.
      B.   Both geese and robins are flying south for the winter.
      C.   Not only geese but also robins are flying south for the winter.

4.   A.   This house and office building will be demolished in June.
      B.   Both this house and this office building will be demolished in June.
      C.   Not only this house but also this office building will be demolished in June.

5.   A.   Ted and his friend delivered newspapers last summer.
      B.   Both Ted and his friend delivered newspapers last summer.
      C.   Not only Ted but also his friend delivered newspapers last summer.

PAGES 207-208:

ANSWERS MAY VARY SLIGHTLY:

1.   A.   The judge and jury left the courtroom suddenly.
      B.   Both the judge and jury left the courtroom suddenly.
      C.   Not only the judge but also the jury left the courtroom suddenly.

2.   A.   The real estate agent and her clients looked at the house.
     B.   Both the real estate agent and her clients looked at the house.
     C.   Not only the real estate agent but also her clients looked at the house.

3.   A.   The Renoir and Monet paintings were being shown at a museum.
     B.   Both the Renoir and Monet paintings were being shown at a museum.
     C.   Not only the Renoir painting but also the Monet painting were being shown at a museum.

4.   A.   The wedding ceremony and reception will be held in the hotel's garden.
     B.   Both the wedding ceremony and reception will be held in the hotel's garden.
     C.   Not only the wedding ceremony but also the reception will be held in the hotel's garden.

PAGES 209-210:

ANSWERS MAY VARY SLIGHTLY:

1.   The hungry teenager ate popcorn, pretzels, and chips.
2.   The doctor examined the patient's throat, ears, and nose.
3.   Our mechanic placed the pliers into the tool box and the jack into the trunk.
4.   Her speech should have been longer and more detailed.
5.   A cheerleader yelled loudly, energetically, and enthusiastically for his team.
6.   Janelle, the errand person, forgot to go to the post office and to pick up a package at a retail store.
7.   Josh may leave at noon, at 2 P. M., or at midnight.
8.   Calculators are usually accurate, easy to use, and convenient.

PAGES 211-212:

ANSWERS MAY VARY SLIGHTLY:

1.   Jeannie enjoys knitting, horseback riding, and playing tennis.
2.   Our neighbor is adventuresome, intelligent, and creative.
3.   His aunt listened patiently and sympathetically.

LEVEL 2 ANSWERS: ITEMS IN A SERIES

4. The family took a camera, a blanket, and fishing poles to the lake.
5. A major corporation decided to hire more employees, to train a receptionist, and to promote two supervisors.
6. The caverns are filled with stalagmites, stalactites, and impressive pools of water.
7. Broccoli, brussel sprouts, and carrots contain beta carotene.
8. The young actress starred in a musical, a drama, and a comedy hit.
9. The short poem was interesting, amusing, and well-written.

PAGE 214:

ANSWERS MAY VARY SLIGHTLY:

1. Both Dalmatians and St. Bernards are named for geographic locations.
2. A naval vessel sailed both the Atlantic Ocean and the Mediterranean Sea.
3. His presentation was both expressive and impressive.

1. Wundt was not only a psychologist but also a physiologist.
2. Breonna is not only president of her class but also president of the drama club.

PAGE 216:

ANSWERS MAY VARY SLIGHTLY:

1. The postal employee is both efficient and agreeable.
2. The family went to both a museum and an observatory last Saturday.
3. The youth group presented both a religious play and a concert.

1. Peoria is not only a city in central Illinois but also the name of an Arizona town.
2. The child not only screamed loudly but also threw himself on the floor.

PAGE 217:

ANSWERS MAY VARY SLIGHTLY:

1. The lake is oblong or oval.
2. The caverns are sixty or seventy feet below the earth's surface.

3.   These chairs have been manufactured by Dawson Industries or Endel Enterprises.
4.   Their mother has been in the U. S. Army or Navy.
5.   On weekends, Mark enjoys mountain climbing or spelunking.

PAGE 219:

ANSWERS MAY VARY SLIGHTLY:

1.   The young woman needs to purchase a jacket or a long coat.
2.   I may go to the beach or to the mountains next Tuesday.
3.   Her little brother wants a wagon or a tricycle for his birthday.
4.   The gold watch had been made in Germany or in Switzerland.

PAGES 221-222:

ANSWERS MAY VARY SLIGHTLY:

1.   Janelle's boss gave her either a bouquet of tulips or a basket of carnations as a birthday gift.
2.   Courtney told either her aunt or her uncle a hilarious story.
3.   Josh gave his grandmother either a necklace or a bracelet.
4.   Sally Alexander wants to become either a computer analyst or an accountant.
5.   Mrs. Johnson has flown either to Miami or to Chicago for a business trip.

PAGES 223-224:

ANSWERS MAY VARY SLIGHTLY:

1.   Mr. and Mrs. Winters have sent either apricots or oranges to their former neighbors.
2.   Rebecca has applied for admission either to a state university or to a community college.
3.   Bruce and Robyn want to become either physicians or medical assistants.
4.   His manner of speaking can be either very pleasant or, at times, extremely churlish.
5.   The leader has given either the top club member or the top two club members awards.

LEVEL 2 ANSWERS: ITEMS IN A SERIES

PAGES 225-226:

ANSWERS MAY VARY SLIGHTLY:

1. Neither the cargo ship nor the oil tanker has arrived.
2. Either a piece of kelp or a jellyfish has floated to shore.
3. Clark broke either his ankle or the tibia in his leg.
4. Neither the essay winner nor the science fair winner had been announced.
5. Either the photographer or her assistant will take your picture now.
6. Either Sue or her brothers are in a hurry.
7. Neither William nor his cousin can go to the stadium tonight.
8. Either the boys or their mother will be coming to the performance.
9. Either the nurses or the doctors are not ready for surgery.

PAGES 227-228:

ANSWERS MAY VARY SLIGHTLY:

1. Swimming is fun, but water skiing is more exciting.
2. Brett will ride the rapids first, and his sister will follow.
3. You may take the garbage out now, or you may wait until after dinner.
4. Miss Blake was hired for the job, and her first day will be tomorrow.
5. An alligator surfaced at the water's edge, but it did not come near our canoe.
6. Your science report may be written, or it may be presented orally.
7. The building had been started six months earlier, but rain had slowed construction.
8. Mrs. Jones is mayor of our city, and Mr. Jones is a councilman.
9. Mail was delivered at noon, but her check was not in it.
10. The cast iron skillet contained frying bacon, and in a kettle, oatmeal bubbled.
11. Cindy will earn fifty dollars for her trip, or she can't go.

PAGES 229-230:

ANSWERS MAY VARY SLIGHTLY:

1. Megan purchased a camera, but she did not buy any film.
2. Timothy may attend Shippensburg University, or he may join the Marine Corps.
3. Both cockateels and cockatoos are colorful Australian birds, but cockatoos are predominantly white.

LEVEL 2 ANSWERS: ITEMS IN A SERIES

4. Uncle Fred is a financial consultant, and Aunt Jane is a journalist.
5. A slight earthquake occurred, but it was felt only by a few people.
6. The pinball machine has broken, but Dad thinks he can repair it.
7. Mr. Kennedy will move to Atlanta this week, and his family will join him after the school year has ended.
8. You may clean the garage today, or you may wait until tomorrow.
9. Hannah joined an archaeological dig, and she said that it was a thoroughly enjoyable experience.
10. His physician suggested Cecil lose weight, or he could be a prime candidate for a heart attack.

LEVEL 2 ANSWERS: SEMICOLON CONSTRUCTION

PAGES 235-236:

1.	NC	4.	NC	1.	+		
2.	C	5.	NC	2.	-		
3.	NC	6.	C	3.	+		
		7.	NC	4.	+		
		8.	NC				
		9.	NC				
		10.	NC				
		11.	C				
		12.	C				
		13.	NC				
		14.	C				
		15.	NC				

PAGES 237-238:

ANSWERS MAY VARY SLIGHTLY:
REPRESENTATIVE ANSWERS:

1. Peter plays baseball for the A's; his championship game is today.
2. Jim's dad is a carpenter; his mom is a real estate agent.
3. Lunch will be at one o'clock; therefore, you may not go out to play.
4. Their sister had a tonsillectomy; however, she was not hospitalized long.
5. You must wake tomorrow at 5 A.M.; therefore, it is wise for you to go to bed early.
6. His uncle works for a dairy; his aunt stays home with three small children.
7. A large, leafy plant stood in the corner of the room; beside it was a marble statue of Caesar.
8. The purse was made of fine leather; however, it has been badly stained.
9. The painting is an original Renoir; therefore, it is very valuable.

PAGES 239-240:

ANSWERS MAY VARY SLIGHTLY:
REPRESENTATIVE ANSWERS:

1. She burned her little finger; however, the injury was minor.
2. The clown made funny faces; therefore, the audience laughed.

LEVEL 2 ANSWERS: SEMICOLON CONSTRUCTION

3.   Milly was hungry; therefore, she bought three hot dogs.
4.   The kitten chased a butterfly; however, she soon lost interest.
5.   Toby hit the ball to first base; however, he was called out.
6.   He cut his finger; therefore, a small bandage was placed around it.
7.   They ran out of gas; therefore, they had to walk two miles.
8.   A glass fell on the floor; however, it didn't break.
9.   Gregg rides his bike to school; therefore, his mom bought him a lock for safeguarding it.

PAGE 241:

ANSWERS MAY VARY SLIGHTLY:
REPRESENTATIVE ANSWERS:

1.   A sailboat glided swiftly by; our small boat was no match.
2.   A frown covered his face; he realized he had left his book at home.
3.   Janelle swims nearly every day; therefore, she will try out for a local swim team.
4.   The table is piled high with food; please feel free to serve yourself.
5.   Construction has begun on the home; a cement foundation was poured yesterday.
6.   The car was badly damaged; however, fortunately, no one was injured.

PAGES 243-244:

ANSWERS MAY VARY SLIGHTLY:
REPRESENTATIVE ANSWERS:

1.   The referee raised both hands; therefore, we knew our team scored a touchdown.
2.   Karen finished first; therefore, she helped others who were having difficulty with the assignment.
3.   The fashion show was a success; however, the dresses were very expensive.
4.   The prospectors searched for gold for three months; however, they didn't find a major vein in the abandoned mine.
5.   A leak had been found in the water pipe; therefore, Opal and Ted replaced the pipe.
6.   A championship game will be played today; therefore, our family will watch it on television.

444

LEVEL 2 ANSWERS: SEMICOLON CONSTRUCTION

7.   That horse is the one the Fremont family likes best; however, its racing days are over.

PART II

1.   The President of the United States spoke on television; therefore, most regularly televised programs had been interrupted.
2.   The building had been badly damaged during a hurricane; however, it was worth salvaging due to its historical significance.

PAGES 245-246:

ANSWERS MAY VARY SLIGHTLY:
REPRESENTATIVE ANSWERS:

1.   The carpet cleaning company has finished the task; therefore, no one should walk on the wet carpet.
2.   Large, pointed rocks stuck out of the water's surface; therefore, we carefully maneuvered our canoes through the treacherous area.
3.   Kyle's brother just received his driver's license; however, he doesn't have his own car.
4.   A pile of bricks lay in their front yard; workmen had been hired to build a low wall.
5.   The flight from Boston arrived at 2 P. M.; however, the one from Chicago was running an hour late.
6.   A baby crawled through some autumn leaves; his mother watched carefully that he didn't try to eat them.
7.   A cheese and potato casserole had been placed on the table; vegetables and breads had been set near it.
8.   The phone had been disconnected; however, the phone service gave out the new number.
9.   A large tornado was spotted in the area; the service station attendant quickly boarded all the station's glass windows.
10.   A new restaurant will open next Tuesday; let's go to its grand opening.

Activity: *ANSWERS WILL VARY.*

LEVEL 2 ANSWERS: APPOSITIVES

PAGES 251-252:

ANSWERS MAY VARY SLIGHTLY:

1. The director, **Tom Lang**, is head of the Movie Institute.
   Tom Lang, **the director**, is head of the Movie Institute.
   The head of the Movie Institute, **Tom Lang**, is the director.
2. My aunt, **Lydia C. Cameron**, flew to Tahiti.
   Lydia C. Cameron, **my aunt**, flew to Tahiti.
3. My brother, **Mark**, is on the basketball team.   (no comma necessary but acceptable)
   Mark, **my brother**, is on the basketball team.
4. Janelle, **my cousin**, is wearing a blue dress.
   My cousin, **Janelle**, is wearing a blue dress.
5. That ring, **an emerald**, is my grandmother's.
   That ring, **an emerald one**, is my grandmother's.
6. Maria, **a good athlete**, likes soccer best.
7. This doll, **an antique**, is over one hundred years old.
   This antique, **a doll**, is over one hundred years old.

PAGES 253-254:

ANSWERS MAY VARY SLIGHTLY:

1. John Davis, **president of Diet Enterprises**, presents seminars about weight loss.
   The president of Diet Enterprises, **John Davis**, presents seminars about weight loss.
2. A cobra, **a poisonous snake**, lives in Asia or Africa.
3. Daniel Boone, **a famous frontiersman**, blazed the trail into Kentucky.
   A famous frontiersman, **Daniel Boone**, blazed the trail into Kentucky.
4. Eagerly Janet read the note, **an invitation to a party**.
5. A history exam, **one all Blake High School students dread**, will be given Monday.
6. Martin's brother, **the recipient of a scholarship**, will attend a nearby university.

LEVEL 2 ANSWERS: APPOSITIVES

7.   Professor Daines wrote three children's books, **all award winners**.
8.   Peggy, **an outstanding cheerleader**, won the state championship for cheering.

PAGES 255-256:

ANSWERS MAY VARY SLIGHTLY:

1.   Ms. Johnson, **director of a women's organization**, planned a fashion show.
      Director of the women's organization, **Ms. Johnson**, planned a fashion show.
2.   The keys fell into the pit, **a hole twenty feet deep**.
3.   The thoroughbred, **winner of the race**, is owned by the Wilson family.
      The winner of the race, **a thoroughbred**, is owned by the Wilson family.
4.   Her hair, **a mass of curls**, needs to be trimmed.
5.   Sam Jones, **my neighbor**, made two touchdowns during last night's game.
      My neighbor, **Sam Jones**, made two touchdowns during last night's game.
6.   Vincent Van Gogh, **a famous artist**, was a friend of Claude Monet.
      A famous artist, **Vincent Van Gogh**, was a friend of Claude Monet.
7.   Please give this to my brother, **the one holding two balloons**.
8.   Mom brought flowers, **petunias and daisies**, for the pot.

PAGES 257-258:

ANSWERS MAY VARY SLIGHTLY:

1.   Janes' dad, **a dentist**, talked to us about dental care.
2.   The Christmas tree, **a six-foot pine**, was decorated with red lights and silver tinsel.
      A six-foot pine, **a Christmas tree**, was decorated with red lights and silver tinsel.
3.   Please hand me that magazine, **the one with the President's picture on the front**.
4.   The house, **a run-down shack**, was over eighty years old.

LEVEL 2 ANSWERS: APPOSITIVES

5.   Nick Gillette, **an apprentice carpenter**, works for his uncle's construction company.
      An apprentice carpenter, **Nick Gillette**, works for his uncle's construction company.
6.   Her hair was twisted in a multi-level braid, **a new style**.
7.   The Strait of Gibralter, **an opening into the Mediterranean Sea**, is approximately thirty-five miles long.
8.   Mr. Jones arrived with Lucy Morrow, **the town librarian**.

LEVEL 2 ANSWERS: PRESENT PARTICIPLE CONSTRUCTION

PAGES 263-264:

1. laughing
2. chasing
3. lifting
4. giving
5. staying
6. going
7. believing

ANSWERS WILL VARY:
REPRESENTATIVE ANSWERS:

1. laughing for ten minutes
2. talking to his brother
3. walking down a dusty road
4. leaving at 5 P. M.
5. exploring a cave
6. designing a house

ANSWERS WILL VARY:
REPRESENTATIVE ANSWERS:

1. Stopping suddenly, the car left skid marks.
2. Dribbling a basketball, Peter ran down the court.
3. Climbing down the steep mountain, each person was very cautious.
4. Playing a game, five children darted after a blue ball.

PAGES 265-266:

1. driving
2. hitting
3. playing
4. finishing
5. throwing
6. sending
7. living

ANSWERS WILL VARY:
REPRESENTATIVE ANSWERS:

1. calling to his friend
2. chasing some thieves
3. lifting weights
4. giving directions
5. staying home
6. going to the river
7. believing the worst

ANSWERS WILL VARY:
REPRESENTATIVE ANSWERS:

1. Jumping into the pool, Heidi splashed her sister.
2. Standing in line, Mrs. Dillard read a mystery.

LEVEL 2 ANSWERS: PRESENT PARTICIPLE CONSTRUCTION

3.   Pulling on a rope, Seth dragged a concrete-filled bucket across the muddy lawn.

PAGES 267-268:

ANSWERS WILL VARY:
REPRESENTATIVE ANSWERS:

1.   Making a bed, the twins tucked in the sheets.
(These may, of course, be written differently. Example: Tucking in the sheets, the twins made the bed.)
2.   Sniffing the floor, the dog searched for food.
3.   Preparing a salad, the chef added ripe tomatoes.
4.   Playing in the sand, the children are making a sand castle.
5.   Sailing on rough waters, the boat suddenly capsized.
6.   Making faces at her little brother, Jamie tries to scare him.

PAGES 269-270:

ANSWERS WILL VARY:
REPRESENTATIVE ANSWERS:

1.   Running down the hall, the girl tripped on her shoelace.
2.   Watching television, her dad ate popcorn.
3.   Standing in line, the lady read a book.
4.   Bathing her dog, Jenny rubs shampoo on the dog's fur.
5.   Frying chicken, Dad is getting ready for a picnic.
6.   Throwing a tantrum, the little girl stuck her tongue out at us.

PAGES 271-272:

ANSWERS WILL VARY:
REPRESENTATIVE ANSWERS:

1.   Serving the volleyball, Jane balanced the ball on her fingertips.
2.   Baking a cake, Charlie set the timer.
3.   Singing very loudly, the gentleman drew attention and stares.

LEVEL 2 ANSWERS: PRESENT PARTICIPLE CONSTRUCTION

4. Repairing his bike, Edward removed the wheel with a wrench.
5. Jumping up and down, the kindergartners shouted with delight.
6. Tripping over a toy, Sarah Jean made her way across the playground.
7. Declaring her innocence, the young lady murmured and began to cry.
8. Preparing for a hurricane, the coastal town offered several shelters.
9. Finding someone's lost puppy, the Harpers searched for its owner.
10. Scolding their little brother, they shook their finger at him.
11. Pushing a shopping cart, Mr. Lopez wandered through the store.

PAGES 273-274:

ANSWERS WILL VARY:
REPRESENTATIVE ANSWERS:

1. Waiting for a bus, Brad drew pictures in the dirt.
2. Drawing a funny picture, the cartoonist chuckled to himself.
3. Choosing partners, the students learned to square dance.
4. Discussing their holiday plans, the Brown family realized they didn't have enough time for a long trip.
5. Leaning against the wall, the juvenile waited for his buddy.
6. Realizing her mistake, Claudia returned to the pharmacy to retrieve her credit card.
7. Standing in front of a mirror, Lynette combed and brushed her long, wavy hair.
8. Writing a check, Garth showed his identification card.
9. Walking their dog, Jamie and Roberta admired the scenery.

PAGES 275-276:

ANSWERS WILL VARY:
REPRESENTATIVE ANSWERS: ***Refer to the note on the next page.***

1. The huge castle, standing against the side of a mountain, is five hundred years old.
2. Five cheerleaders, yelling loudly, led their team onto the field.
3. The cat, sleeping peacefully by the fire, startled the lady who nearly sat on him.
4. The rooster, standing in a small, fenced yard, crowed loudly.
5. The hair stylist, cutting hair all day, often stops to answer the phone.
6. The boy, cleaning his room, listens to the radio.

LEVEL 2 ANSWERS: PRESENT PARTICIPLE CONSTRUCTION

PAGES 277-278:   *Refer to the note at the bottom of this page.*

ANSWERS WILL VARY:
REPRESENTATIVE ANSWERS:

1. The player, running down the court, passed the ball.
2. The bee, buzzing around the room, landed on the table.
3. Her dad, driving very fast, braked quickly to avoid hitting an animal in the road.
4. The motorist, looking very sad, is checking the dent in her new car.
5. A large boat, sliding against a rock, overturned.
6. Sandy, looking at the envelope suspiciously, checked the postmark.
7. The flag, blowing in the wind, is our club's banner.

PAGES 279-280:   *Refer to the note at the bottom of this page.*

ANSWERS WILL VARY:
REPRESENTATIVE ANSWERS:

1. Her sister, laughing hysterically, held her side.
2. A black ant, crawling on the sidewalk, stopped a moment, changed directions, and continued his march.
3. Her red balloon, floating toward the fluffy clouds, had been released with a shout.
4. A pig, eating greedily, paid no attention to the farmer.
5. A customer, looking for a white suit, was thrilled to find it on sale.
6. The well-dressed lady, touching the gold necklace, admired its unique design.
7. The governor, presenting a speech, emphasized the need to combat drugs.
8. A stallion, prancing proudly, entered the horse show arena.
9. Her long hair, falling softly against her face, was full of static.
10. A little green frog, hopping along the pool of water, croaked energetically.
11. One lone, quiet man, sitting on the beach, watched the breaking waves.
12. A large vase of flowers, tilting precariously against two candlesticks, caught my eye.

Note: There is disagreement about commas.   Many believe that the commas aren't needed if the phrase is integral to the sentence meaning.

452

LEVEL 2 ANSWERS: PRESENT PARTICIPLE CONSTRUCTION

PAGES 281-282:

ANSWERS WILL VARY:
REPRESENTATIVE ANSWERS: **Refer to the note on the previous page.**

1. A small squirrel, cracking a minute nut, scanned the area for intruders.
2. His big brother, wearing a toga, left for a Roman festival.
3. A fawn, lying by its mother, lifted its head.
4. The minister, reading a passage of scripture, paused, looked at the congregation, and continued in a more emphatic tone.
5. A tired mother, lifting two bags of groceries from the car, sighed wearily.
6. Her favortie uncle, wearing a tuxedo, escorted her down the aisle.
7. A policeman, making his rounds, had discovered the robbery.
8. Their pet parakeet, sitting on Todd's shoulder, chirped loudly.
9. A store clerk, wrapping the sweater in tissue, suggested a matching skirt.
10. A small brown snake, slithering through some tall weeds, silently approached its prey.
11. That tall man, asking a service station attendant for directions, is rather confused.
12. The farmer, planting corn, has solicited help from his neighbors.
13. A busy secretary, making several copies, absentmindedly pushed the wrong button.

PAGE 283:

ANSWERS WILL VARY:
REPRESENTATIVE ANSWERS:

1. Praying
2. Purring
3. Swerving
4. Dribbling
5. Watching
6. Pacing
7. Smiling

LEVEL 2 ANSWERS: PRESENT PARTICIPLE CONSTRUCTION

PAGE 285:

ANSWERS WILL VARY:
REPRESENTATIVE ANSWERS:

1. Frowning
2. Blushing
3. Whispering
4. Freezing
5. Cheering
6. Agreeing
7. Shivering
8. Nodding

PAGE 287:

ANSWERS WILL VARY:
REPRESENTATIVE ANSWERS:

1. Frowning, Joe examined the scratch on his truck.
2. Resting, the elderly couple sat on a park bench.
3. Barking, the lonely dog darted toward the fence.
4. Laughing, Brett played a trick on his mom.
5. Running, the traveler crossed the airline terminal.
6. Coughing, the patient reached for some medication.
7. Falling, I felt foolish and embarrassed.

PAGE 289:

ANSWERS WILL VARY:
REPRESENTATIVE ANSWERS:

1. Yawning, he stretched both arms over his head.
2. Standing, the crowd sang the national anthem.
3. Crying, Donna watched the movie's ending.
4. Stopping, a limousine driver motioned for pedestrians to cross the street.
5. Listening, her father nodded to his friend.

454

LEVEL 2 ANSWERS: PRESENT PARTICIPLE CONSTRUCTION

6.   Smiling, the bride and groom exchanged wedding vows.
7.   Limping, a football player left the field as the crowd applauded him.

PAGES 291-292:

ANSWERS WILL VARY:
REPRESENTATIVE ANSWERS:

1.   Shopping is terrific fun for some people.
2.   Talking on the telephone is necessary in his real estate ventures.
3.   Skiing is not only enjoyable but also very good exercise.
4.   Earning an excellent grade in math is Glenda's major goal this semester.
5.   Running became Troy's manner of releasing tension.
6.   Traveling to a foreign country can be costly.
7.   Riding a bicycle was very difficult for the child who was trying to learn without using training wheels.
8.   Going to the lake for the day is our family's favorite summer activity.
9.   Picking cotton was a long and tedious job for many Southerners.

PAGES 293-294:

ANSWERS WILL VARY:
REPRESENTATIVE ANSWERS:

1.   Playing a sport can teach cooperation and teamwork.
2.   Doing dishes was boring until John began to play with the bubbles.
3.   Sleeping out under the stars was a new experience for them.
4.   Getting a traffic ticket did not help to improve my day.
5.   Washing a car is the teenager's idea of fun.
6.   Going on vacation can be exhausting.
7.   Laughing at the comedienne's jokes made our sides hurt.
8.   Taking a test for which one has studied is not usually stressful.
9.   Finding gold is Uncle Steve's lifetime ambition.

LEVEL 2 ANSWERS: PAST PARTICIPLE CONSTRUCTION

PAGES 299-300:

1.	cooked	11.	decorated
2.	started	12.	finished
3.	practiced	13.	driven
4.	eaten	14.	departed
5.	brushed	15.	given
6.	bought	16.	sold
7.	scored	17.	polished
8.	swum	18.	agreed
9.	run	19.	shaken
10.	pasted	20.	cried

PAGES 301-302:

1.	helped	9.	repaired
2.	sung	10.	seen
3.	flown	11.	gone
4.	parked	12.	smelled
5.	called	13.	drunk
6.	stolen	14.	watched
7.	broken	15.	chosen
8.	looked		

PAGES 303-304:

1. (had) delivered
delivered goods
2. (had) preferred
preferred customers
3. (had) cancelled
a cancelled check
4. (had) disappointed
the disappointed child
5. (had) wasted
wasted time
6. (had) frightened
a frightened animal
7. (had) digested
digested food
8. (had) relaxed
a relaxed person
9. (had) horrified
the horrified woman
10. (had) demanded
a demanded bribe
11. (had) inherited
an inherited estate
12. (had) occupied
occupied territory

LEVEL 2 ANSWERS: PAST PARTICIPLE CONSTRUCTION

PAGES 305-306:

1. (had) rejected
   a rejected offer
2. (had) postponed
   a postponed game
3. (had) annoyed
   an annoyed person
4. (had) furnished
   a furnished apartment
5. (had) purified
   purified water
6. (had) established
   an established company
7. (had) changed
   changed behavior
8. (had) forgotten
   a forgotten message
9. (had) dimmed
   dimmed headlights
10. (had) announced
    the announced meeting
11. (had) screened
    a screened porch
12. (had) worried
    a worried mother

PAGES 307-308:

1. an embarrassed person — Embarrassed, Tom's face turned bright red.
2. a confused secretary — Confused, the secretary frowned.
3. a determined young woman — Determined, Joanna pushed harder against the rock.
4. softened butter — Softened, the butter was ready to be added to the batter.
5. an agitated customer — Agitated, the customer again explained why she didn't want the product.
6. a forgotten watch — Forgotten, the watch lay by the sink for three days.
7. a confused motorist — Confused, the motorist exited the freeway.

PAGES 309-310:

1. a secured boat — Secured, the boat rocked idly in the water.
2. a stalled vehicle — Stalled, the vehicle blocked the intersection.
3. a cherished ring — Cherished, the antique ring was kept in a velvet-lined case.
4. a saturated cloth — Saturated, the cloth dripped gravy all over the floor.

457

LEVEL 2 ANSWERS: PAST PARTICIPLE CONSTRUCTION

5.   a restricted area   Restricted, the area was off limits to everyone but army personnel.

6.   a remodeled house   Remodeled, the house was worth twice its original value.

7.   a fascinated toddler   Fascinated, the toddler watched the fireworks burst across the night sky.

PAGES 311-312:

ANSWERS WILL VARY:
REPRESENTATIVE ANSWERS:

1. Frustrated, the driver sat in traffic for twenty minutes.
2. Matted, the dog's coat was hard to brush.
3. Cornered, the frightened raccoon clawed at its attacker.
4. Hidden, a camera flashed the shopper's picture.
5. Discouraged, the math teacher realized the concept had not been mastered.
6. Freed, a tiny butterfly fluttered away.
7. Distracted, Amy and Marcus stopped playing their board game.
8. Surprised, she smiled and hugged her grandmother.
9. Worried, the physician examined the X-ray again.

PAGES 313-314:

ANSWERS WILL VARY:
REPRESENTATIVE ANSWERS:

1. Contented, his baby brother snuggled against his mother.
2. Delighted, the young woman purchased two novels.
3. Frightened, a small yellow bird flew against a window.
4. Disgusted, the journalist slammed down his pencil and rubbed his eyes.
5. Troubled, Mr. Grange asked to see the manager.
6. Preoccupied, a young mother ran the stroller into the counter.
7. Elated, her brother waved a banner as his team raced for a touchdown.
8. Amazed, the crowd watched the acrobats perform.
9. Puzzled, the little boy tilted his head to look under the toy.

LEVEL 2 ANSWERS: PAST PARTICIPLE CONSTRUCTION

PAGES 315-316:

ANSWERS WILL VARY:
REPRESENTATIVE ANSWERS:

1. Given extra time to do the project, Claude continued to work on a physics experiment.
2. Disturbed by a large phone bill, the father threatened to remove the telephones.
3. Placed on top of a shelf, the package, long forgotten, gathered dust.
4. Purchased for a dollar, the key chain glowed in the dark.
5. Lifted from swirling water, the flood victim was resuscitated.
6. Terrified by a loud scream, I ran into an alley and hid.
7. Discovered by a talent agent, Miss Barnes traveled to Nashville for an audition.
8. Stranded in the desert, the family called a towing service.
9. Baked for two hours, the cake was burned and hard.

PAGES 317-318:

ANSWERS WILL VARY:
REPRESENTATIVE ANSWERS

1. Stained by red ink, the blouse was soaking in soapy water.
2. Found in a vacant lot, the scrawny kitten needed milk.
3. Warmed by a campfire, the group sang songs and toasted marshmallows.
4. Tired of watching television, the child went outside to play.
5. Urged to do their best, the boys raised money for charity.
6. Written in a hurry, the note was illegible.
7. Exhausted from a long hike, Theda slept for sixteen hours.
8. Freed after the Civil War, the Cross family traveled to Baltimore to begin a new life.

PAGES 319-320:

ANSWERS WILL VARY:
REPRESENTATIVE ANSWERS:

1. Stopped by a policeman, the driver explained that he had not been speeding.
2. Stripped of its old paint, the chest showed wood with deep grains.

459

LEVEL 2 ANSWERS: PAST PARTICIPLE CONSTRUCTION

3. Written at the last moment, the note had been scribbled.
4. Hidden in the shadows, two boys slid further behind the bushes so that they would not be detected during the game.
5. Stuffed inside the desk drawer, some stamped envelopes had been crushed.
6. Prepared by a master chef, the omelet was light and delicious.
7. Finished with their chores, Debra and Francisco walked to the mall.
8. Decorated with streamers and balloons, the banquet room was beautiful.
9. Ridden at a steady gallop, the horses traveled far each day.

PAGES 321-322:

ANSWERS WILL VARY:
REPRESENTATIVE ANSWERS:

1. Given by a men's club, three awards were presented to outstanding students.
2. Started in 1950, the corporation had expanded steadily and had diversified.
3. Found near a hospital, the elderly gentleman apparently needed care.
4. Drawn on a paper sack, the map was difficult to read.
5. Purchased for her friend, Jody's gift reflected kindness and concern.
6. Sent by their companies, the two had met at a Chicago conference.
7. Taken to an emergency room, the child received two stitches.
8. Tackled by a linebacker, the quarterback fumbled the ball.
9. Distracted by a buzzing bee, the woman bumped into a picnic table.

PAGES 323-324:

ANSWERS WILL VARY:
REPRESENTATIVE ANSWERS:

1. Selected as the winner, Mira's jam received a blue ribbon.
2. Fastened to a sled, five bright flags flapped in the wind.
3. Scored by the team's slowest runner, the goal was hailed by everyone.
4. Dissolved in warm water, the yeast was activated.
5. Kept neatly in Dan's immaculate workroom, the saws were easy to find.
6. Returned to the sender, the letter contained important documents.
7. Hurled into the air, the disk landed on the soft green grass.
8. Teased by passing pedestrians, the dog snarled.
9. Dressed casually in shorts and shirt, the couple is going to the park.

LEVEL 2 ANSWERS: PAST PARTICIPLE CONSTRUCTION

PAGES 325-326:

ANSWERS WILL VARY:
REPRESENTATIVE ANSWERS:

1. The girl, taken by surprise, laughed at the bad news.
2. This cup, broken into several pieces, needs to be repaired.
3. Their father, given an award by the mayor, was thrilled.
4. The rose bush, planted in the fall, bloomed during the spring.
5. The book, dedicated to Mr. and Mrs. Harrison, is a children's book about Holland.
6. The Statue of Liberty, restored for our nation's celebration, stands proudly in New York Bay.
7. The bride, given in marriage by her father, wore a trailing white gown with a sequined bodice.
8. The telephone bill, received at the end of the month, always lists long distance calls separately.
9. His answer, said in a loud voice, startled everyone.
10. A large bear, disturbed by a loud crash, charged into the forest.
11. The guest, greeted at the door by the hostess, presented a basket of fruit.
12. Ice cream, thawed for an hour, is much too soft.
13. The cave, discovered recently, will open to the public within three years.

PAGES 327-328:

ANSWERS WILL VARY:
REPRESENTATIVE ANSWERS:

1. Frank's mother, known for her great cookies, received an award for her molasses squares.
2. The automobile, stalled in the middle of the street, slowed traffic immensely.
3. Mary's party, attended by twenty of her friends, was held at a local ethnic restaurant.
4. Mr. Pratt, born in Canada, is a member of this town's civic organization.
5. Our neighbor, disguised as an elf, visited five nursing homes.
6. The story, released to the press, related information concerning the governor's campaign for re-election.
7. Jack's response, whispered to a friend, drew attention to them.

8. The last guest, delayed by a snowstorm, took off his boots and snow-covered jacket.
9. An egg, protected by a thin shell, is a very fragile object.
10. The antique rocker, inherited from their grandmother, was placed in the family room.
11. The clothing, manufactured in Maine, was made for skiing.
12. Her idea, presented to the group, was well received.

LEVEL 2 ANSWERS: HAVING + PAST PARTICIPLE CONSTRUCTION

PAGE 333:

Note: The answer is the same for *A* and *B*.

1.	jumped	7.	walked
2.	waited	8.	broken
3.	talked	9.	picked
4.	found	10.	said
5.	played	11.	fallen
6.	ridden		

PAGE 335:

Note: The answer is the same for *A* and *B*.

1.	blamed	7.	grabbed
2.	read	8.	lifted
3.	given	9.	known
4.	eaten	10.	rung
5.	done	11.	pushed
6.	paused	12.	set

PAGES 337-338:

ANSWERS WILL VARY:
REPRESENTATIVE ANSWERS:

1.	baked	8.	finished
2.	chased	9.	chopped
3.	buzzed	10.	ridden
4.	groomed	11.	tickled
5.	purchased	12.	run
6.	painted	13.	waded
7.	mowed	14.	walked
		15.	written

LEVEL 2 ANSWERS: HAVING + PAST PARTICIPLE CONSTRUCTION

PAGES 339-340:

ANSWERS WILL VARY:
REPRESENTATIVE ANSWERS:

1.	finished	8.	picked
2.	expressed	9.	dropped
3.	flown	10.	set
4.	purchased	11.	chosen
5.	typed	12.	critiqued
6.	trimmed	13.	lived
7.	gone	14.	known

PAGES 341-342:

ANSWERS WILL VARY:
REPRESENTATIVE ANSWERS:

1. Having written a novel, he contacted a publishing company.
2. Having ridden a motorcycle, the girl dreamed of owning one.
3. Having encountered a general, the officer saluted.
4. Having arranged some flowers, the florist sent them immediately.
5. Having fished for a day, the children were excited.
6. Having earned some money, they bought tickets to a game.
7. Having won the case, the attorney smiled at his client.
8. Having removed a cast, the doctor examined the patient's foot carefully.
9. Having watched Phillip's reaction, his mother grinned.

PAGES 343-344:

ANSWERS WILL VARY:
REPRESENTATIVE ANSWERS:

1. Having completed a painting of a dragon, the artist entered it in an art competition.
2. Having dropped her small gift, the exuberant lady became flustered and embarrassed.
3. Having played the game well, the golfer was awarded a cash prize.

464

4. Having learned to be a carpenter, Sam creates beautiful furniture.
5. Having jogged to the store, they were out of breath.
6. Having made chocolate chip cookies, Cindy placed them in a cookie jar.
7. Having tested the new car, their dad decided to purchase it.
8. Having looked at me kindly, the teller completed the transaction.
9. Having seen two plays, the couple ate a late dinner.
10. Having talked with her parents, Lalita chose to watch a different program.

PAGES 345-346:

ANSWERS WILL VARY:
REPRESENTATIVE ANSWERS:

1. Having jumped into the pond, the dog swam around in circles.
2. Having waited for a train for two hours, Mr. Tappan became impatient.
3. Having talked to the coach, Jana decided to try out for the soccer team.
4. Having found a set of keys, Leslie turned them into the office.
5. Having ridden in an antique car, I appreciate the comforts of today's automobiles.
6. Having walked to school, I was late.
7. Having broken a glass, I swept and washed the floor.
8. Having picked up debris around the school, the class was congratulated by an appreciative administrator.
9. Having placed some flowers on the soldier's grave, the couple silently left.
10. Having searched for the lost fisherman, the helicopter returned to its original base.
11. Having tired easily after surgery, he took a nap.
12. Having tried to devour a jelly doughnut too quickly, Jose began to choke.

PAGES 347-348:

ANSWERS WILL VARY:
REPRESENTATIVE ANSWERS:

1. Having asked for a raise, Ms. Begay was pleased with her assertiveness.
2. Having made brownies, Jacy and Lani ate all of them.
3. Having delivered all of the mail, the postal worker headed back to the main terminal.

LEVEL 2 ANSWERS: HAVING + PAST PARTICIPLE   CONSTRUCTION

4.   Having finished the reading assignment, Jacob took notes and studied them.
5.   Having painted his bedroom, Brian hung posters on only one wall.
6.   Having placed the infant in a stroller, the father meandered through the park.
7.   Having discovered America, Columbus was disappointed that he had not found an all-water route to Asia.
8.   Having stapled the papers together, the club's treasurer tallied the year's receipts.
9.   Having prepared the meal, Mr. and Mrs. Levy arranged the china and glassware.
10.   Having swum for two hours, we were tired.
11.   Having earned five dollars, he bought a used book.
12.   Having refused to talk, the journalist was charged with contempt.

PAGES   349-350:

ANSWERS WILL VARY:
REPRESENTATIVE ANSWERS:

1.   Having decided to enroll in the armed services, Tara joined the *WAVES*.
2.   Having recently changed jobs, Don did not take a vacation.
3.   Having used disposable diapers, the Lamsom family found traveling less worrisome.
4.   Having acquired a beach house, Shari spends most weekends surfing.
5.   Having written to his parents, Jacob explained his rationale for his difficult decision.
6.   Having bragged to his friends, the young man realized his error.
7.   Having learned to ski, Danno and Maria ski nearly every winter weekend.
8.   Having given up smoking, we are much happier and healthier.
9.   Having declined the invitation, Lisa sent flowers as a kind gesture.
10.   Having driven through severe hail, the couple was relieved to reach a motel.
11.   Having recently finished college, Joel is now working for a newspaper.
12.   Having received a traffic citation, the young lady must now attend driving school.

466

LEVEL 2 ANSWERS: HAVING + PAST PARTICIPLE CONSTRUCTION

PAGES 351-352:

ANSWERS WILL VARY:
REPRESENTATIVE ANSWERS:

1. Having finished the math test, he checked his work.
2. Having delivered twins, the woman waited patiently to hold them.
3. Having raced his bike in a competition, Frederick realized how much the others had practiced.
4. Having painted her nails, Deka could touch nothing for fear of ruining her manicure.
5. Having lifted an extremely heavy box, Martin has injured his back.
6. Having bought a puppy, our family spent free moments entertaining it.
7. Having taken several pictures, I chose the best for the project.
8. Having gone sledding, the children happily slid out of their wet jackets.
9. Having learned to use the computer, John rarely uses a typewriter.
10. Having tried unsuccessfully to ski, Wendy lay on her back and moaned
11. Having been a policeman, Mr. Decker finds his detective experience beneficial in private detective work.
12. Having washed the dog, Emma stood back as the dog jumped from the tub.
13. Having written many books, he has become quite famous.

PAGES 353-354:

ANSWERS WILL VARY:
REPRESENTATIVE ANSWERS:

1. A bus driver, having spoken to the unruly youngster previously, took him to the principal.
2. Her favorite aunt, having retired last year, travels frequently.
3. This jacket, having down filling, is quite warm.
4. Carole and Bart's dad, having been a professional football player, is in great shape.
5. My friend, having made the honor roll, went to an awards dinner.
6. That duck, having waddled aimlessly for two hours, appears lost.
7. Their dentist, having filled two of Regina's teeth, suggested that flouride treatments be given.
8. The nice clown, having performed for the small children, handed out balloons.

LEVEL 2 ANSWERS: HAVING + PAST PARTICIPLE CONSTRUCTION

9.   A tiny baby, having cried for nearly an hour, was taken to an emergency room.
10. Mr. and Mrs. Wilson, having two sons in Africa, will spend the holidays alone this year.
11. Three scuba divers, having taken their first dive, were extremely enthusiastic.
12. A fawn, having heard a noise, moved closer to its mother.

PAGES 355-356:

ANSWERS WILL VARY:
REPRESENTATIVE ANSWERS:

1.   The fisherman, having caught a small fish, threw it back.
2.   Jack's foot, having been stepped on, was bruised.
3.   This old building, having been condemned, will be demolished.
4.   A chocolate bar, having melted, was smeared on the leather seat of her car.
5.   The coach, having practiced with the team a long time, dismissed everyone.
6.   Their Siamese kitten, having green eyes, is lovely.
7.   Jake, having lifted weights for a year, has large muscles.
8.   A tall, burly waiter, having tripped, spilled soup on a customer.
9.   A group of firemen, having returned from a call, rested.
10. These towels, having been thrown into an empty locker, smell putrid.
11. Many alligators, having been killed, were used for purses.

LEVEL 2 ANSWERS: SUBORDINATE CLAUSES

PAGES 361-362:

1. DC
2. DC
3. IC
4. DC
5. IC
6. DC
7. DC
8. IC
9. DC
10. IC
11. DC
12. IC
13. IC
14. DC
15. IC
16. IC
17. DC
18. IC
19. DC
20. IC

PAGES 363-364:

1. IC
2. IC
3. DC
4. DC
5. IC
6. IC
7. DC
8. DC
9. DC
10. IC
11. DC
12. IC
13. DC
14. IC
15. DC

LEVEL 2 ANSWERS: SUBORDINATE CLAUSES

16. IC
17. DC
18. IC
19. IC
20. DC

PAGE 366:

ANSWERS WILL VARY:
REPRESENTATIVE ANSWERS:

1. Whenever a scientist makes an extraordinary discovery, he often writes about it in a scholarly magazine.
2. After a hurricane swept the coast, removal of debris began immediately.
3. Although his reaction was nonchalant, I could tell that he was deeply troubled.
4. Before a lawyer may practice law in a state, he must take a special examination.
5. While a trapeze artist climbed a ladder, her partner swung high above the crowd.
6. Until the package is wrapped, keep it in a closet.
7. Since you insist on discussing the matter, let's be calm.
8. If paramedics are summoned, they usually arrive within ten minutes.

PAGE 368:

ANSWERS WILL VARY:
REPRESENTATIVE ANSWERS:

1. While Mr. Harkins lived in Italy, he visited many cathedrals.
2. Although their father enjoyed the depths of the sea when scuba diving, he detested flying.
3. Before the tornado was reported in the vicinity, his family had been picnicking.
4. Whenever the farmer needed fresh vegetables, he simply went out to his garden.
5. If your brain is affected by drugs, you cannot think rationally.
6. Because an explorer discovered a strait at the tip of South America, it is named after him, the Strait of Magellan.
7. As the policeman motioned the car to proceed, another vehicle nearly hit him.

470

LEVEL 2 ANSWERS: SUBORDINATE CLAUSES

PAGES 369-370:

ANSWERS WILL VARY:
REPRESENTATIVE ANSWERS:

1.   While Dr. Baxter examined the patient, her nurse prepared a vaccine.
2.   If that corporation closes, one can expect a recession.
3.   Although Candace hesitated and sighed, her energy level began to return.
4.   As the mountain climber reached the summit, his companions prepared to raise a flag.
5.   If one receives an anonymous phone call, it's advisable to tell someone in authority.
6.   When a local mechanic repaired George's automobile, his bill was reasonable.
7.   After William earned a degree, he worked for his father's business.
8.   Even though the committee met several times, no decisions were reached.
9.   While Janelle distributed papers, her sister asked customers for donations for the needy.
10. Before Americans won their independence, this country belonged to the British Empire.

PAGES 371-372:

ANSWERS WILL VARY:
REPRESENTATIVE ANSWERS:

1.   After the goat fled from the barn, two sheep followed.
2.   When the team ran onto the field, the crowd cheered ecstatically.
3.   If the lemons are fresh, please squeeze enough for a quart of juice.
4.   Before the man boarded the train, he checked his briefcase again.
5.   Whenever the baby cries, both parents pace the floor.
6.   Because rain fell in torrents, her coat was soaked.
7.   When they arrived, Tamra and Chessa immediately called home.
8.   Until you learned to walk, your crawling probably had become rather fast.
9.   While some children played hide-and-seek, others watched.
10. Wherever the horse gallops, its colt follows.

LEVEL 2 ANSWERS: RELATIVE CLAUSES

PAGE 378:

ANSWERS WILL VARY:
REPRESENTATIVE ANSWERS:

1. A telegram that Mom has saved was sent by her grandfather.
2. An Indian tribe which lives in the Southwest is Papago.
3. Their youth director who is from the East introduced them to hoagies.
4. Some flowers that had been planted in the spring are now blooming.
5. A house which is over a hundred years old was bought for a mere thousand dollars.
6. An ocean liner which will sail tomorrow has to be inspected again.
7. My neighbor who goes to the beach each summer collects shells.
8. The man whom I met earlier walked into the dining room.

PAGE 380:

ANSWERS WILL VARY:
REPRESENTATIVE ANSWERS:

1. Beige stationery that she had imprinted was her gift.
2. The aunt whom we love is coming to visit soon.
3. Martin's son who sings with a barbershop quartet will perform tonight.
4. The model whose picture appeared in a fashion magazine earns a large sum of money.
5. The cardboard box which he put under the bed contains old family pictures.
6. The teacher whose class won a reading contest was given a set of novels for the classroom.
7. A state senator who spoke to the women's club headed an educational committee.
8. The postal lady whom Mrs. Perkins likes gave us a large manila envelope.

PAGES 381-382:

ANSWERS WILL VARY:
REPRESENTATIVE ANSWERS:

1. The teacher called names that began with R.

472

LEVEL 2 ANSWERS: RELATIVE CLAUSES

2. An accident which occurred on the freeway was not a serious one.
3. Tony gave the paper to Susan who suddenly handed it back to him.
4. The run-down mill which is located on Larkin Road is for sale.
5. Brian is a senior to whom a scholarship was given.

PAGE 384:

ANSWERS WILL VARY:
REPRESENTATIVE ANSWERS:

1. His niece who graduated from Bucknell University earned her graduate degree from Northern Arizona University.
2. A white latticed arch that was delivered to the church was covered with white lilies and pink roses.
3. The little boy gave his mother a hand-painted noodle necklace which he had made in preschool.
4. A tall, dignified judge whom I had met during another case entered the courtroom.
5. The man whose son won the Indianapolis 500 had been a famous race car driver.

PAGES 385-386:

ANSWERS WILL VARY:
REPRESENTATIVE ANSWERS:

1. The first grader who checked out a library book was extremely proud.
2. This silver dollar that dates back to the early 1890's is valuable.
3. The puzzle which a young lady bought is missing two pieces.
4. A child whose parents are involved with his activities is, quite definitely, fortunate.
5. The decision that Frances Marie made pleased everyone.
6. An idea which was formulated by their uncle had been purchased by a major oil company.
7. She gave the medicine to the nurse whose intensive care experience was trusted.
8. Samantha bought a notebook that included a dictionary and thesarus in the back.

9. James's suggestion which was approved by the city council led to the planting of Christmas pines in public parks.
10. We talked to a detective who had interviewed several witnesses.
11. A business partner whose children are in school frequently rearranges her schedule to accommodate them.

PAGES 387-388:

ANSWERS WILL VARY:
REPRESENTATIVE ANSWERS:

1. Mr. Kemper's nephew who is an engineer designed this bridge.
2. The emerald ring that the jeweler polished was exquisite.
3. The checking account which was overdrawn needed a hundred dollars added to it.
4. The speaker who delivered the commencement speech was both profound and funny.
5. Her homework that had been left on the kitchen table became the cat's litter paper.
6. The point which Mrs. Little had been trying to make was relevant to the committee's proposal.
7. The baby whose mother is Norwegian has blue eyes and blonde hair.
8. The rug that their family bought is a Persian masterpiece.
9. A pianist who has entered this competition is from Japan.
10. His wishes which had been stated clearly in his will reflected a concern for humane treatment of all animals.
11. The customer who forgot her credit card, most likely, will return for it.